Navajo Weavings

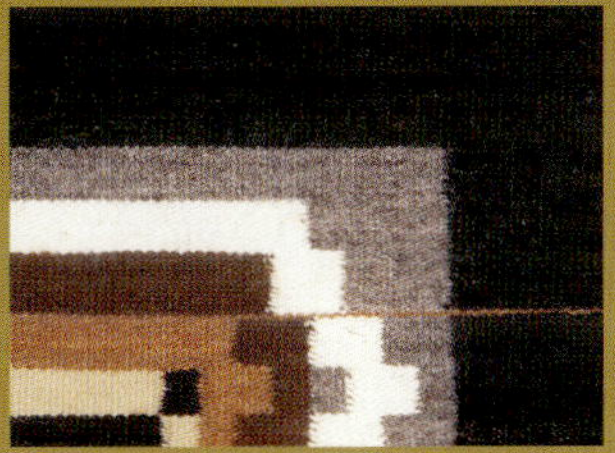

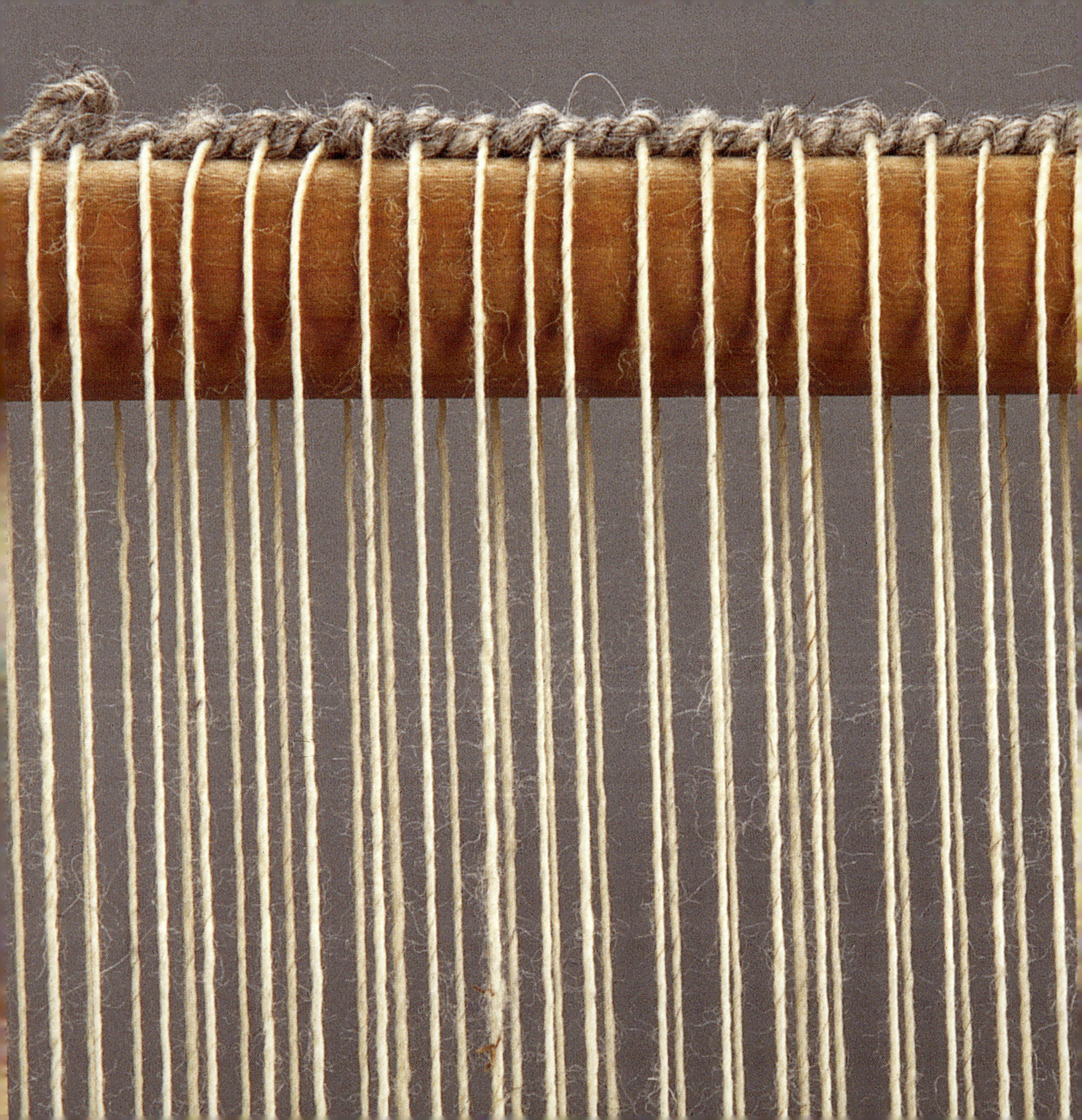

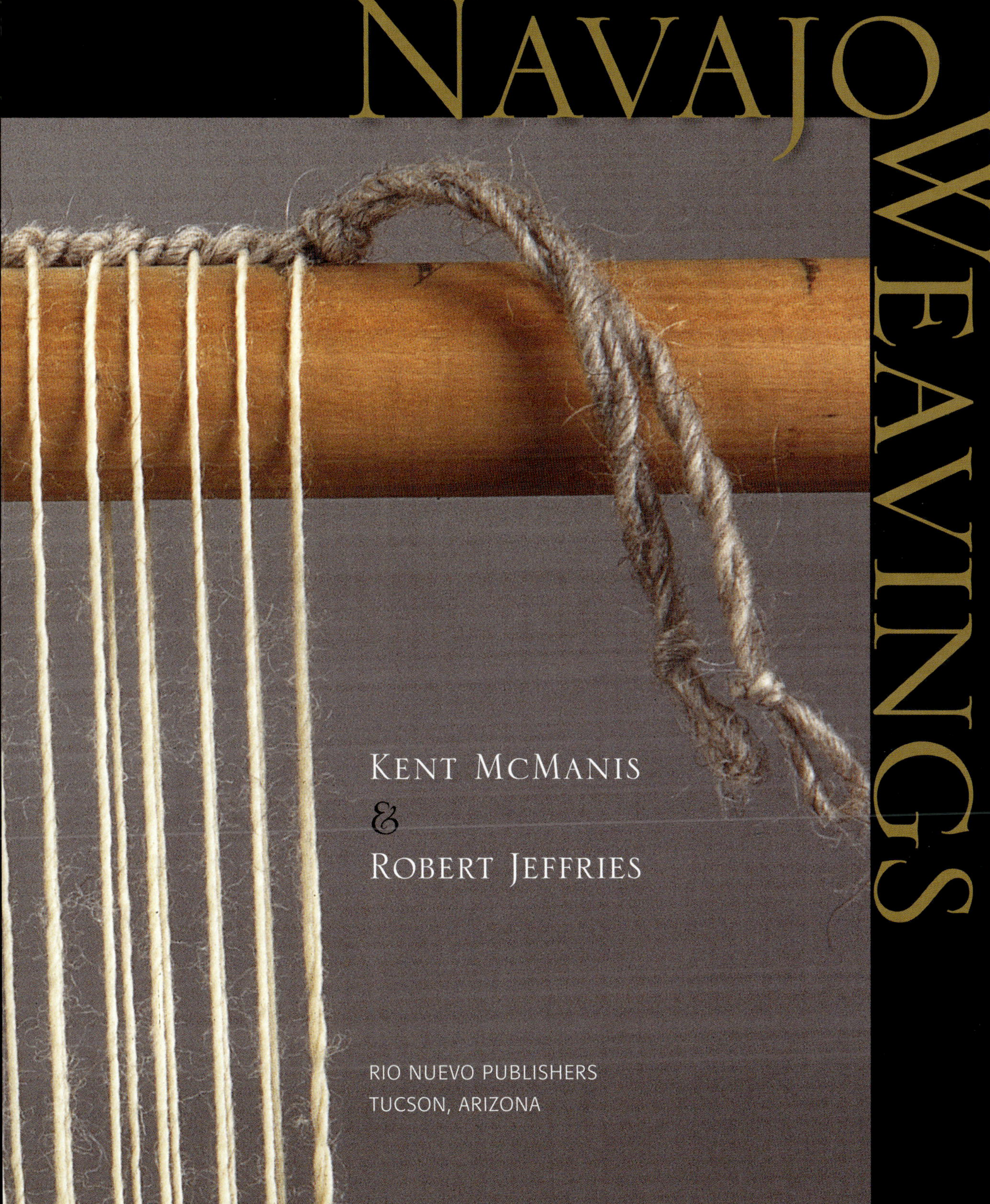

NAVAJO WEAVINGS

Kent McManis
&
Robert Jeffries

RIO NUEVO PUBLISHERS
TUCSON, ARIZONA

Rio Nuevo Publishers®
P.O. Box 5250
Tucson, AZ 85703-0250
www.rionuevo.com

Photography credits as follows:
Robin Stancliff: Front and back covers; Pages 1, 2–3, 7, 10, 13 bottom, 14, 16, 20, 21 top, 23, 26, 27, 29–32, 34–36, 38, 40, 41, 43, 44, 46, 47, 48 top, 49–52, 53 bottom, 54–56, 62, 63, 65, 69, 76–85, and 89.
W. Ross Humphreys: Pages 6, 13 top, 15, 17–19, 21 bottom, 22, 24, 28, 33, 37, 39, 42, 45, 48 bottom, 53 top, 59, 61, 70, 73, 74, 86, 87, and 90.

Map on page 12 by Karen Schober.
Illustration on page 58 by Jessica LeMar.

On the front cover: Navajo loom with partially completed weaving by Katherine Cleveland.
On the back cover: Yé'ii Bicheii weaving by Daisy Nakai (top); third-phase chief's blanket variation, circa 1865 (bottom).

Rugs courtesy of Shiprock Trading Company: Page 10; Figures 17, 21, 23, 24, 29, 30, 31, 32, 41, 46, 48, 62, 63, and 66.
Rugs courtesy of Twin Rocks Trading Post: Figures 27, 43, 68, and 69.
Rugs courtesy of Blair's Dinnebito Trading Post: Figures 45, 70, and 71.
Rugs courtesy of Terry De Wald: Figures 2, 3, 9, and 14.
Rugs courtesy of private collections: Page 6; Figures 1, 4, 5, 6, 7, 8, 11, 12, 18, 19, 25, and 35.
All other rugs are courtesy of Grey Dog Trading Company.

Library of Congress Cataloging-in-Publication Data

McManis, Kent.
Navajo weavings / Kent McManis and Robert Jeffries. -- 2nd ed.
    p. cm.
Rev. ed. of A guide to Navajo weavings. 1997.
Includes bibliographical references and index.
ISBN-13: 978-1-933855-36-3 (pbk. : alk. paper)
ISBN-10: 1-933855-36-3 (pbk. : alk. paper)
1. Navajo textile fabrics. I. Jeffries, Robert. II. McManis, Kent. Guide to Navajo weavings. III. Title.
E99.N3M5155 2009
746.7'2--dc22

                                    2009027030

Book Design: Karen Schober, Seattle, Washington

Printed in Korea.

10 9 8 7 6 5 4 3 2 1

Acknowledgments

*We wish to thank many people for their help with this project.
First, we would like to thank Laurie McManis for her patience, many
suggestions, and hard work without which we could not have completed the book.
Special gratitude goes to Jed Foutz for his enthusiastic encouragement, extra efforts,
and friendship and to Bruce McGee for his continued support and
uncommon kindness. Our appreciation also goes to Bruce Burnham,
Kent Morrow, Stephen Pickle, Robert Ingeholm, Georgianna Kennedy Simpson,
Jackson Clark II, and Bill Malone for their invaluable information. Extra special
thanks to Terry DeWald for his help on older weavings.
As always, kudos to Robin Stancliff for her special talents.
Also to Ross Humphreys for the new photos. Our heartfelt thanks to all the weavers
who have so generously shared their knowledge of weaving techniques and their
personal histories with us over the years. And last but not least, we owe a
special debt of gratitude to Barbara Teller Ornelas for her input,
time, wisdom, and selfless spirit.*

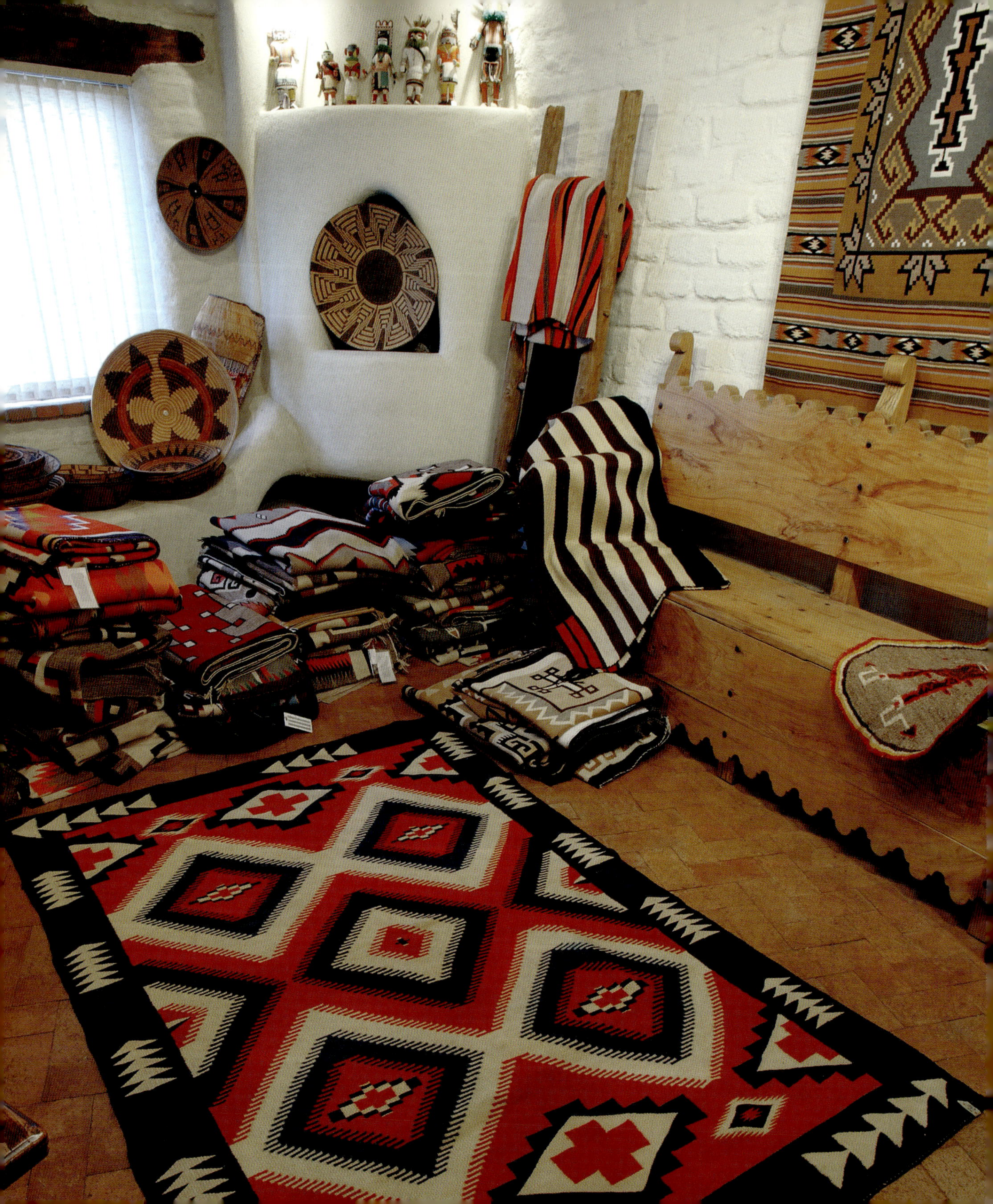

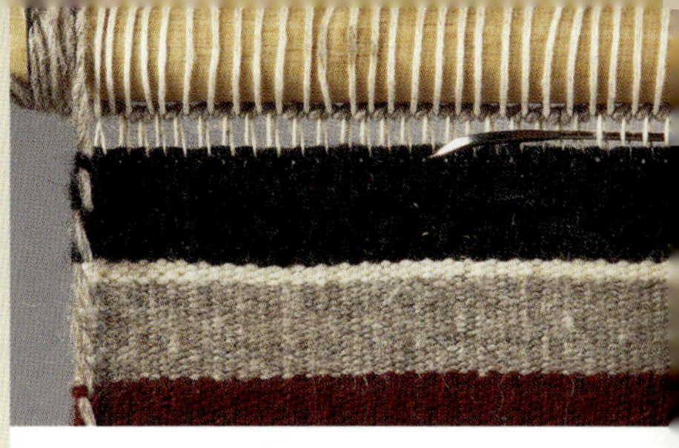

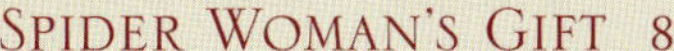

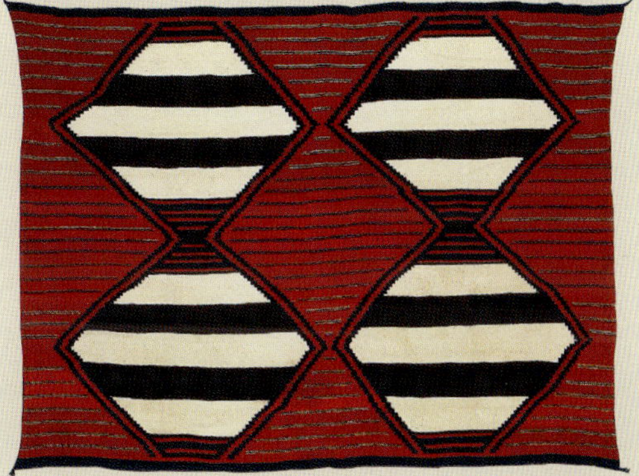

CONTENTS

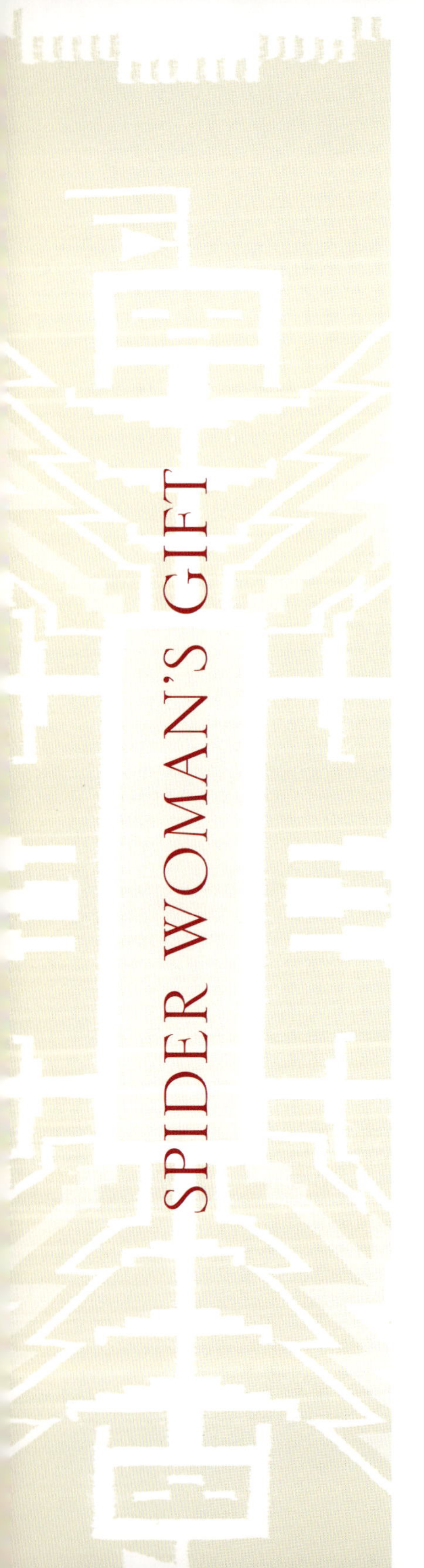

Weaving is at the heart of being
for many Navajo women, an essential
part of their lives that is both vital to
them individually and vital to their
lives within their community.

While hunting and raiding were originally within the man's realm in early times, weaving became primarily the woman's domain. The use of the portable loom allowed a woman to tend her sheep, watch her children, and weave simultaneously. Over the years, weaving came to play a crucial role in female relationships and in instilling shared values and structure in the Navajo community. As such, this skill has become a source of personal pride for the Navajo woman and enhanced the respect from her people. Its practitioners today still perpetuate their tribal traditions while reflecting a dramatically transformed way of life.

The Navajos believe that the gift of weaving was taught to them by Spider Woman, one of the Navajo Holy People. Spider Woman originally showed Changing Woman (another Holy Person) how to weave, with the stipulation that she would in turn teach the Navajo. Spider Man showed them how to make the loom and tools out of sacred Navajo stones and shells (turquoise, jet, white shell, and abalone), as well as with the earth, sun, rain, and sky themselves. This important connection to the earth and elements is characteristic of the Navajo respect and reverence for the natural world. It also demonstrates the significance of weaving within the Navajo religion.

Along with the belief in the sacred origin of weaving, many Navajos give credence to specific taboos. While a number of younger weavers no longer follow them and some beliefs seem purely localized, many weavers still heed these traditions. The weavers of some regions still incorporate the famous spirit trail, or weaver's pathway, near the finish of their rugs (See "The Art of the Navajo Loom" chapter). Many artists feel that designing rugs with Navajo deities, called *Yé'ii* (YEH-ee), snakes, or bears is sacrilegious. Setting down tools while weaving or leaving tools in the loom when not weaving is believed by some to bring misfortune. Some weavers don't weave at night; some don't weave while pregnant. Some think it unacceptable to joke about weaving, seeing it as a serious endeavor. Some weavers sing songs about their rugs while weaving to ensure success. Many also pray before, during, and after creating a piece to aid their current work and future success.

While weaving itself may not be intended to perform a specific religious act, it is rooted in the traditions of the Navajo people and therefore imbued with the sacred. Navajo religion revolves around beauty and harmony within their universe; a splendid Navajo rug represents these aspects of their worldview in an appropriately beautiful and lasting form.

The majority of weavers we know today started at an early age, many before they were ten years old. As is typical in a matrilineal society, most weavers learned from their mothers and grandmothers. Some have woven for most of their lives; some go for long periods without weaving. A pattern we have found among several weavers is exemplified by noted artist Barbara Teller Ornelas. As with all traditional Navajo women, Barbara was expected to weave and, although she resisted, was taught to weave by the age of eight by her mother. She experimented occasionally but did not come to fully appreciate and enjoy her ability, however, until years later when her husband, David Ornelas, saw the special quality in her talent and encouraged her to weave full time. Barbara, in turn, has now taught her daughter Sierra and her son Michael her skills.

In the following chapters, we follow the development of Navajo weaving from past to present, tracing how the art has changed over the centuries and where it appears to be headed in the years to come. We also examine how a Navajo rug is made and what to look for when purchasing one. Above all, we hope to convey the respect and appreciation we feel toward Navajo weavers and admiration for their endurance in continuing an art of great beauty.

Overleaf: Navajo loom with partially completed weaving by Katherine Cleveland.

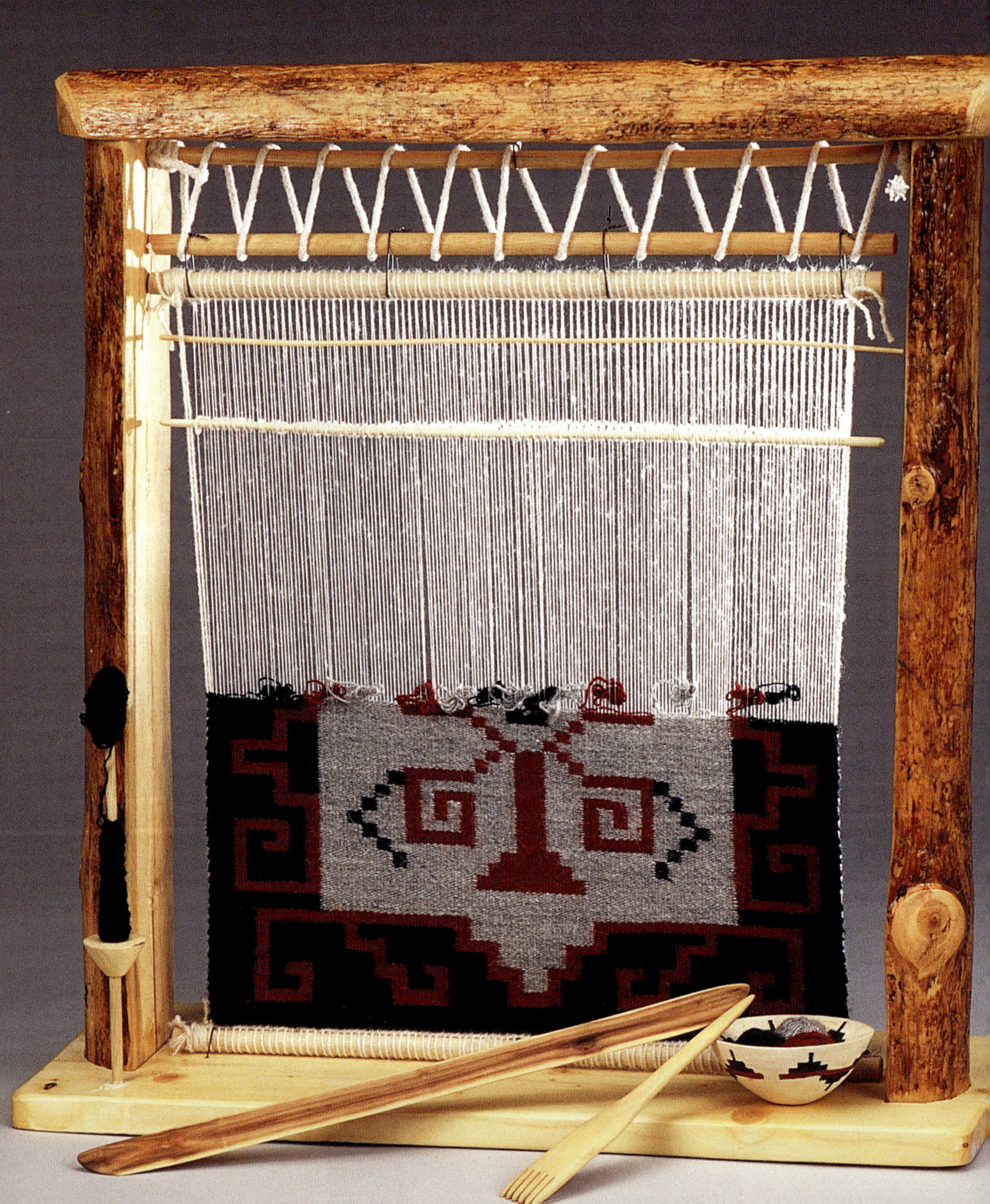

The Navajo call themselves *Diné*
(dih-NEH), meaning "The People."
The word "Navajo" is probably the Spanish
version of the Tewa* word: *navahu*
(*nava* meaning "field" and *hu*
meaning "large arroyo").

This name stems from the fact that some early Navajos farmed large watershed areas in their original northern New Mexico territory.

When did the Navajos arrive in the American Southwest? No two historians or anthropologists seem to agree. It is generally accepted that these Athapaskan-speaking people came sometime between A.D. 1000 and 1500 from western Canada. Their linguistic cousins, the Apache, may have arrived slightly earlier. They were certainly there before the Spanish arrived in the mid 1500s.

The Pueblo Indian peoples had been weaving for several centuries by the time the Navajos appeared in the Arizona-New Mexico region. They wove garments and blankets made of cotton that had been introduced from Mexico by A.D. 800. The Navajos adopted cotton for their own weaving as their Pueblo neighbors taught them the skill. Which Pueblo tribe or tribes were the teachers is unclear. In most pueblos, men were the weavers. However, among the Navajos the art of weaving was originally practiced by women. The cause of this change may have been indirectly brought about by the attempts of the Pueblo peoples to escape the Spanish domination. Primarily during the seventeenth century, many Pueblo people moved away from the Rio Grande Valley region into Navajo territory to the north and west. As the Pueblo and Navajo peoples lived together and undoubtedly

*Tewa (Tay-wah): a Pueblo Indian people and language

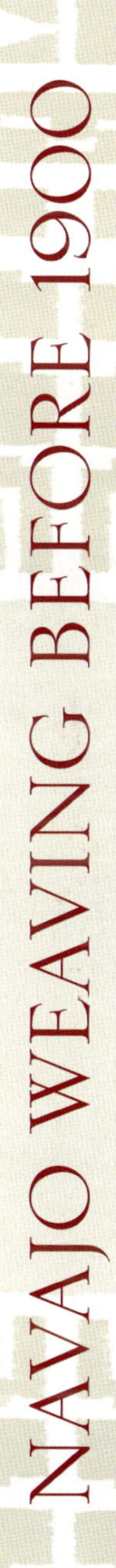

The Navajo Lands consist of an area larger than the state of West Virginia and extend over the Four Corners area of Arizona, New Mexico, and Utah. (The reservation does not cross into Colorado.) The Navajo tribe is the second largest in the country, numbering over 275,000 people.

intermarried, it is easy to see how a Pueblo man could have taught his Navajo wife to weave. The Pueblos temporarily succeeded in the Great Revolt of 1680 against the Spanish, after a century of Spanish demands for tributes and repression of their native religions. After the Spanish reconquest of New Mexico in 1692, even more Pueblo people escaped to the Navajo lands. While the Navajos probably learned weaving in the mid 1600s, Spanish reports verify that they were weaving by 1700. This is considered the beginning of the Classic Period of Navajo weaving.

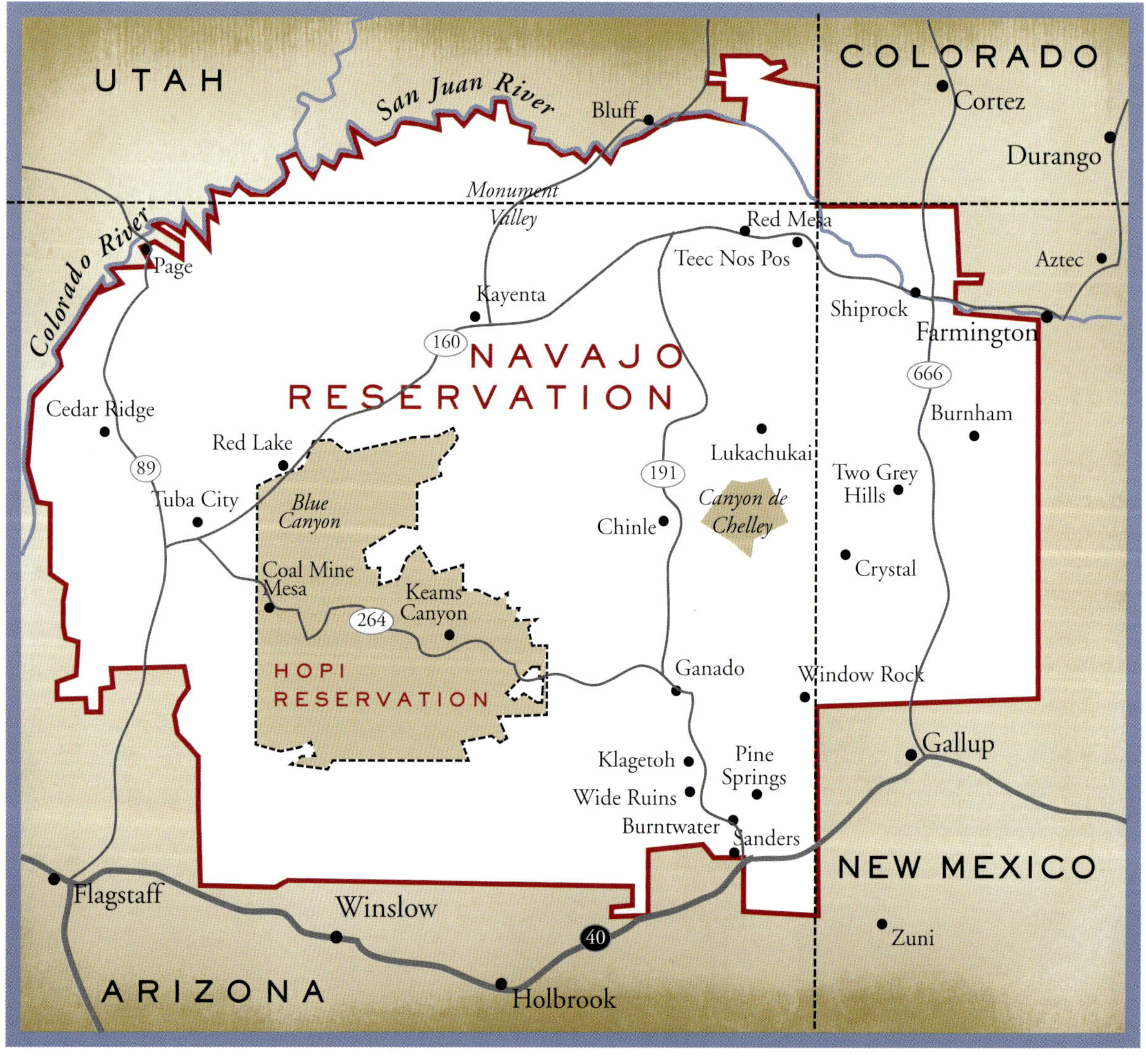

Although Spanish rule was harsh, it introduced certain benefits to the Navajos, most notably the horse and the sheep. The Navajos soon started raiding Spanish settlements to get them. Like other nomadic peoples, the Navajos benefited from the greater mobility of the horse. The sheep gave them both a new food source and a new material for weaving. By 1800, wool had virtually replaced cotton in Navajo textile production.

As the practice of weaving spread, indigo blue dye (derived from the indigo plant) became a popular trade item from the Spanish to the Navajos. Another important item brought by the Spanish was bayeta (by-YET-ah), a wool trade cloth originally from England, where it was called baize. It traveled through Spain to Mexico and then north to New Mexico, first appearing there in the late 1700s. The bayeta was commercially woven and dyed red with either lac (from Old World tree-scale insects) or cochineal (from New World cactus insects). The Navajos did not use the bayeta as it was but raveled it and respun the wool to use in their own weavings.

Mexican independence from Spain in 1821 reversed the protectionist policies of the Spanish government. This allowed new trade channels between the outside

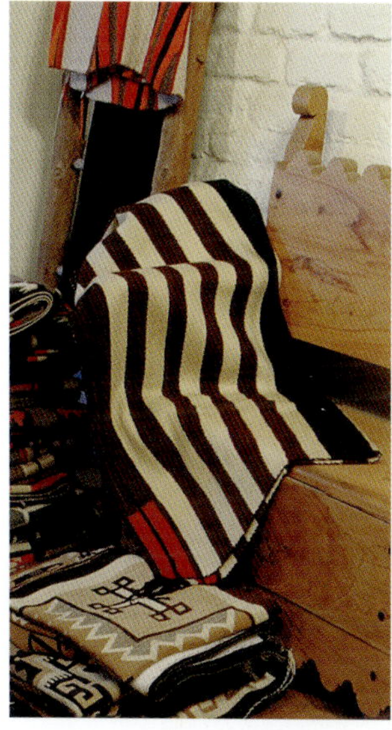

Figure 1 (above). First-phase chief's blanket variation, circa 1875, draped over the bench. The rectangles in the corner of the weaving would not be included in a true first-phase blanket. This blanket has both indigo-dyed blue and aniline-dyed red yarn.

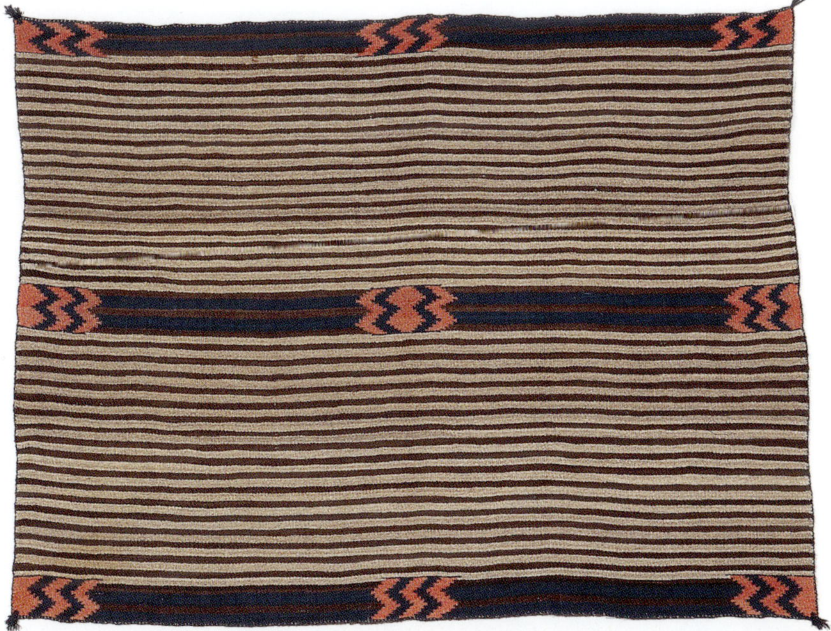

Figure 2 (left). Second-phase chief's blanket variation, circa 1865. 52½ x 40 in. This blanket has zig-zag red areas instead of bars. It was woven using natural grey and brown, cochineal-dyed raveled red, and indigo-dyed blue yarns.

world and the Navajos of the New Mexican Territory. Independence also provided an expanded market for Navajo weavings, including the famed chief's blankets. The name of these blankets was a misnomer, as the Navajos did not have chiefs. But many of these weavings did make their way to powerful and well-to-do Plains Indians. First-phase chief's blankets appeared around 1800 and consisted of a simple, grouped stripe design in indigo, white, and dark brown. (FIG. 1) Before 1850, the second-phase chief's blanket design had added a dozen pairs of red bars to the striped areas. (FIG. 2) Finally, by 1860 the third-phase chief's blanket generally substituted nine whole or partial diamonds to replace the bars. (FIG. 3)

Navajo weavers created many other varieties of wearing blankets and serapes (a wearing blanket that is longer than it is wide) during the Classic Period. (FIG. 4) These included the so-called Moki (MO-kee) blankets, Moki being the Spanish name for Hopi. This style consisted of a dark-brown and indigo-blue striped background on which were superimposed more and more elaborate red designs. While the Navajos undoubtedly copied this striped design from their Pueblo neighbors, the Hopis were not especially known for this particular color scheme in their striped blankets. (FIG. 5)

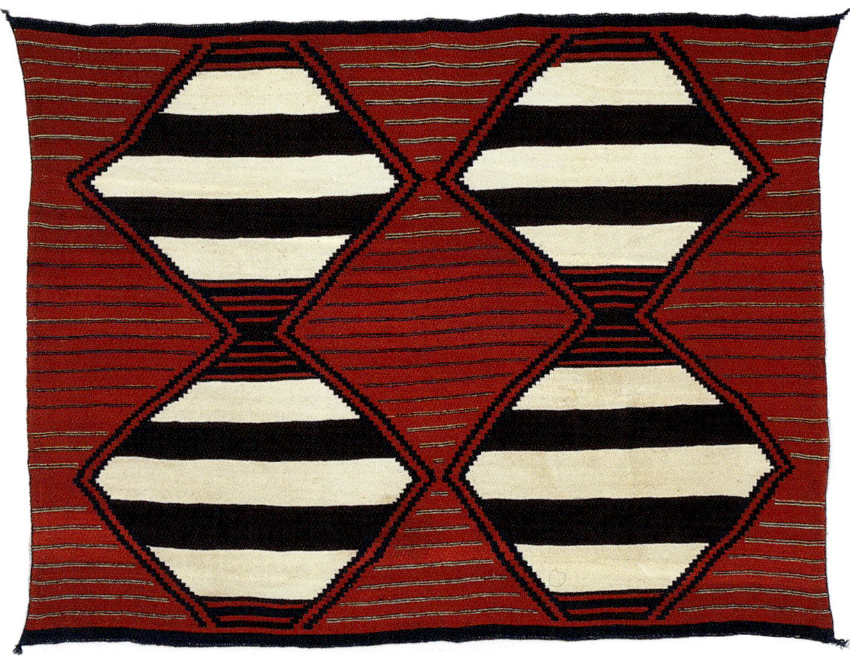

Figure 3. Third-phase chief's blanket variation, circa 1865. 71½ x 54 in. The typical wide background striping is overshadowed by the diamonds in this piece. It was made of natural white and brown, lac- and cochineal-dyed raveled red, and indigo-dyed blue yarns.

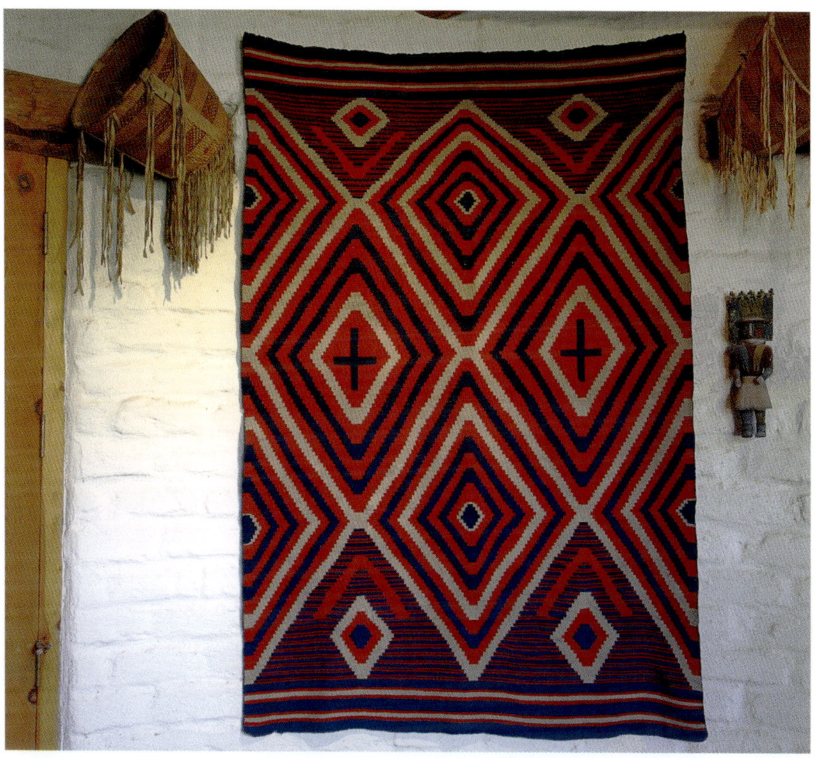

Figure 4. Classic Period serape, circa 1860. This serape has both indigo-dyed blue and cochineal-dyed raveled red yarn (bayeta).

When New Mexico became a United States territory after the Mexican War in 1848, the on-again-off-again raiding between the Navajos and the New Mexicans became an American problem. Unfortunately, the New Mexicans were usually not held accountable for their part in these conflicts as the Navajos were. Several treaties signed between some bands of Navajos and the U.S. Government ended in failure because leaders of these bands had no authority to speak for other Navajos. There was no one leader with whom the Americans could have negotiated to bring all the Navajos together.

In 1863, American forces under Kit Carson began a scorched-earth campaign, destroying the Navajos' crops and slaughtering their sheep. The Navajos were rounded up and forced into confinement at Bosque Redondo near Fort Sumner, New Mexico. Many died on the infamous Long Walk to Fort Sumner, and many more perished of disease while at the internment camp. The government's attempts to induce the Navajos to farm at Fort Sumner failed. Maintenance costs and other problems at the camp became excessive, exacerbated by graft and theft by outsiders. In 1868, the government allowed the Navajos to return to their homeland with a new treaty. Of the over 8,000 Navajos held at Bosque Redondo, over 2,000 had died. The Bosque Redondo debacle is to the Navajo people one of the most tragic and formative episodes in their history.

Several events occurred at Bosque Redondo that would also change the face of Navajo weaving. Along with the Army rations, the Navajos were given blankets produced by the Spanish weavers of New Mexico, blankets with serrated diamond designs derived from the famous Saltillo (sawl-TEE-yo) textiles of northern Mexico. While these diamond elements do appear on Classic Period weavings, they become much more widespread after Bosque Redondo.

The fact that the Navajos had lost almost all of their remaining sheep at Bosque Redondo was another pivotal event. The government replaced about 15,000 sheep and goats as part of the treaty, but with a new breed. Originally, the Navajos raided churro sheep from the Spanish, a breed with long, silky wool that produces a fine yarn for weaving. The Americans replaced them with merino sheep which have short, kinky wool that is greasy and difficult to clean as well as hard to spin and weave. This led to deterioration in the quality of wool available for handspinning: as

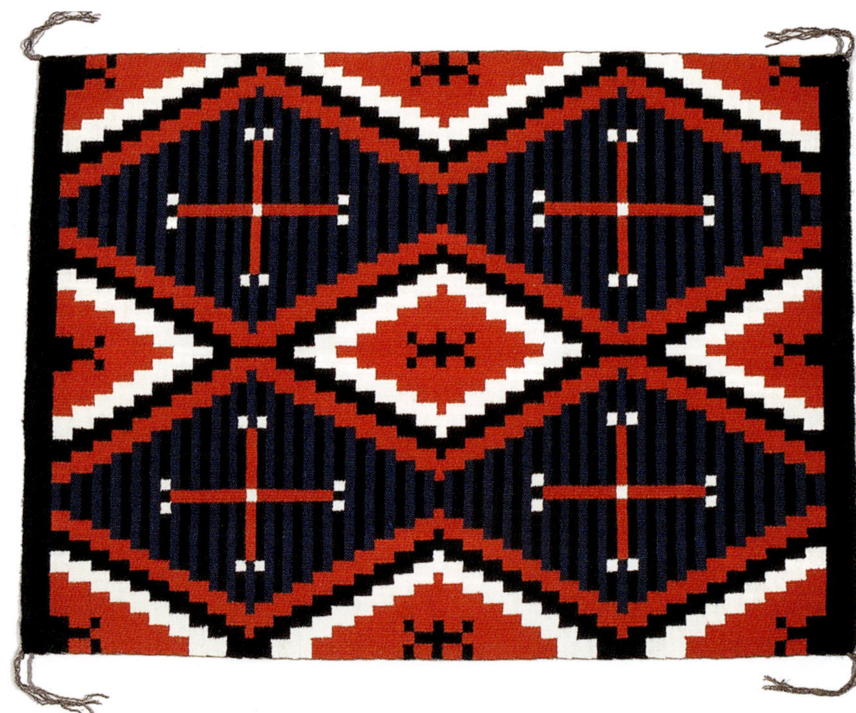

Figure 5. Moki chief's blanket revival tapestry, circa 1990, by Barbara Teller Ornelas. 26 x 18 in. This weaving is a true tapestry with 92 wefts per inch.

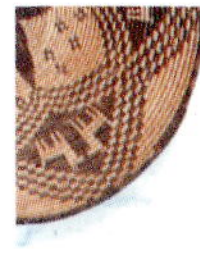

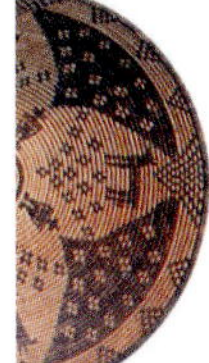

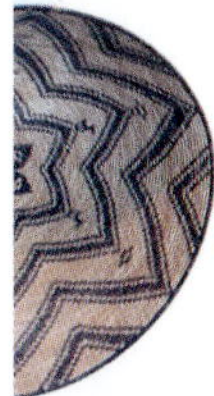

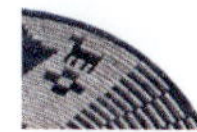

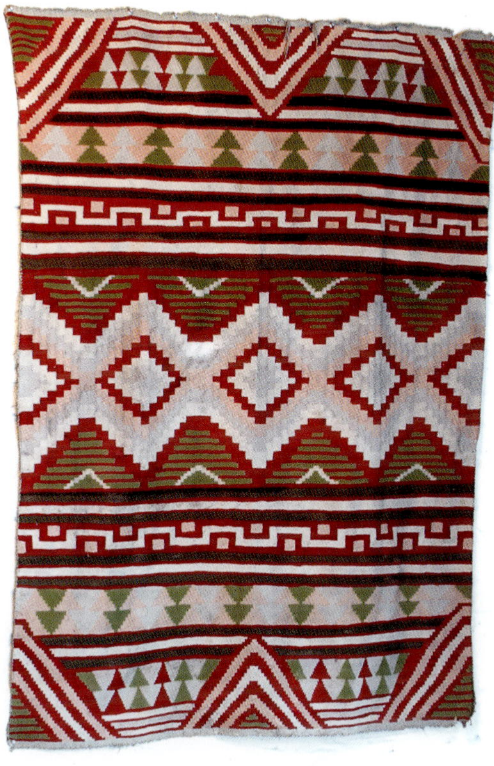

Figure 6. Bosque Redondo Period serape, circa 1865. Woven during the time of the Navajo internment, the yarns are all cochineal-, aniline-, and vegetal-dyed three-ply Saxony yarn.

a result, the Navajos became more and more dependent on commercially spun yarn. From Europe came three-ply Saxony yarn, available before Bosque Redondo along with the bayeta. (FIG. 6) At the camp, Navajo weavers were introduced to commercially spun and dyed, three-ply Germantown yarn. Famous for its many bright colors, it was so named because most of the woolen mills producing it were in or near Germantown, Pennsylvania. This was largely replaced by four-ply Germantown yarn in the 1870s. (FIG. 7, 8, and 9) The deep red cochineal-dyed bayeta cloth was supplanted about this time by aniline-dyed (coal tar dyes), orange-red American flannel. This new cloth was raveled as the bayeta had been. The use of indigo dye also started to diminish and virtually ceased by the 1890s.

All of these changes during or just after Bosque Redondo signaled the end of the Classic Period of weaving and ushered in the Transitional Period. Navajo textiles were changing in several ways. Much of this transformation was brought about by Anglo traders who immediately started setting up operations on or

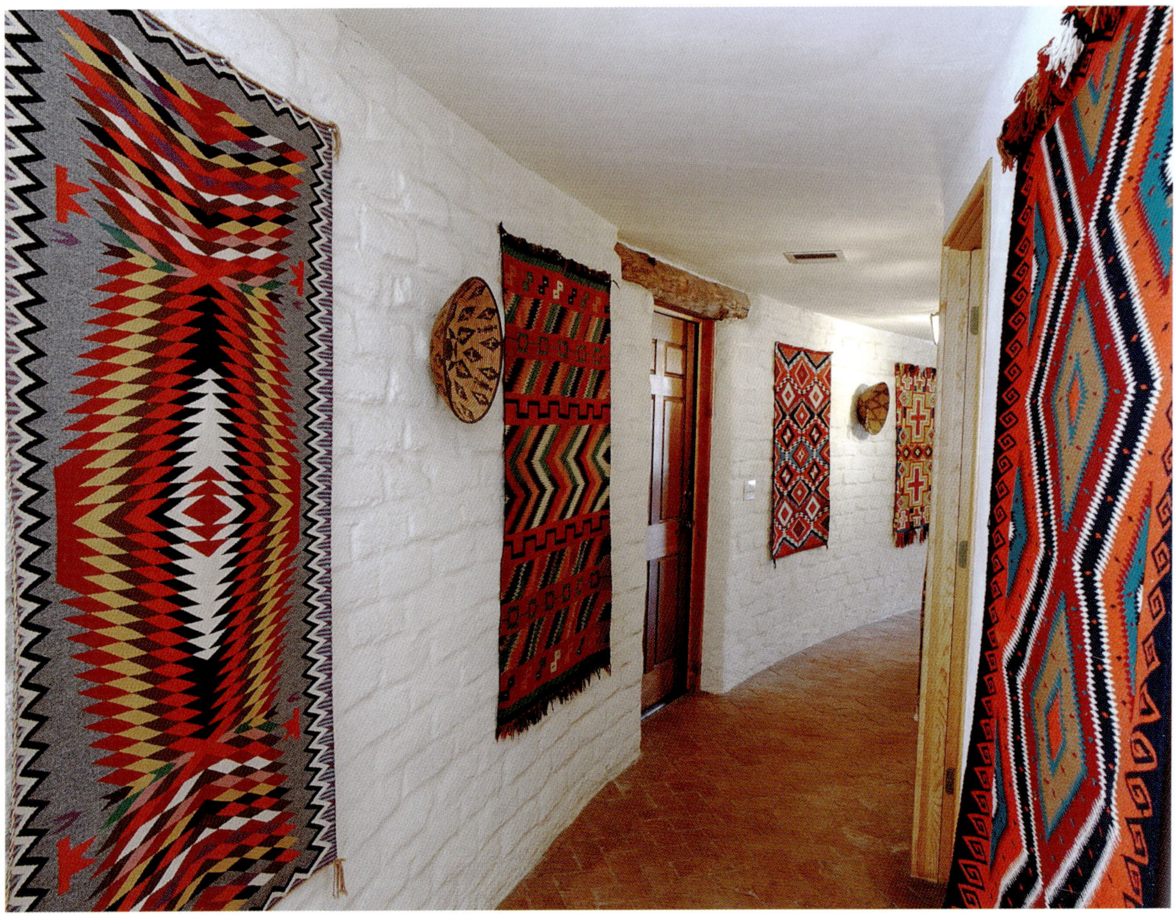

Figures 7 & 8. Germantown weavings, circa 1880–1910, including eye-dazzler patterns (above), and a hand-spun pictorial weaving with Germantown commercial yarn fringe & "balls" (opposite).

around the new Navajo reservation after 1868. They traded coffee and other staples plus, by the late 1870s, individual dye packets that increased the color palette weavers could use in their handspun textiles. In return, the Navajos traded back weavings and wool. The traders soon began to influence the types of weavings produced. Americans wanted floor rugs and decorative weavings rather than blankets to wear. In the 1880s, the arrival of the railroad (and with it, tourists) increased this demand for rugs. Navajo weavers began to use designs with borders to provide the framing effect tourists liked. Serrated pattern, "eye-dazzler" weavings with many vibrant, outlined colors in zig-zag designs became popular. Thus, by the 1890s, Navajo weavings had changed from blankets to rugs and from personal items to saleable trade goods. (FIG. 10 and 11)

Other factors had also begun to affect Navajo weaving. The number of sheep that the government had given to the Navajos had grown to nearly two million. The Pendleton Woolen Mills opened in Oregon in the 1890s, and their relatively inexpensive, commercially made blankets virtually eliminated the need for Navajo-woven blankets. These events led reservation traders to encourage the use of hand-spun wool in weaving (because it was readily available and less expensive than imported, commercially spun yarn) and to concentrate even more on marketing rugs. The most important change was brought about by traders taking a more direct role in improving the quality of Navajo weaving.

One of the first traders to strongly encourage the Navajos to produce higher-quality weavings was Juan Lorenzo Hubbell. Hubbell took over the Ganado (gah-

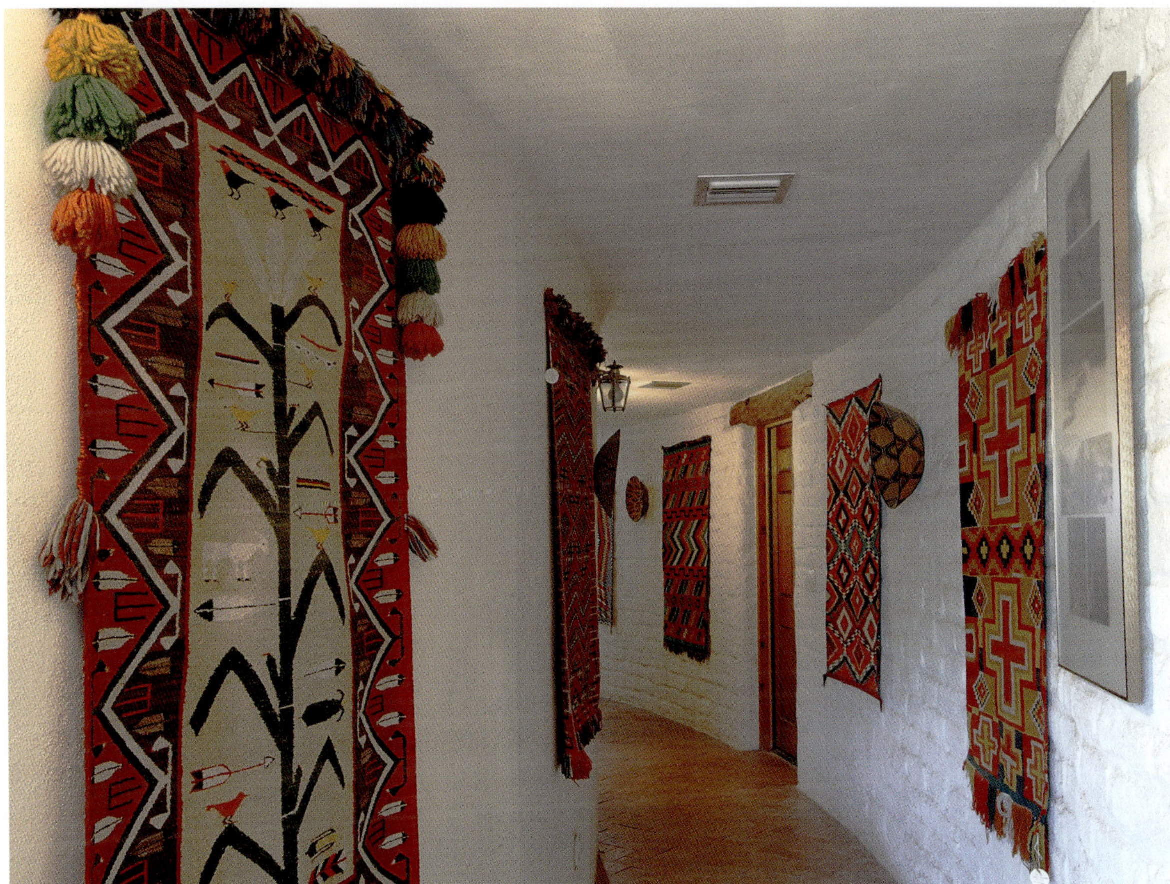

Figure 9. Germantown weaving, circa 1880. 53 x 36 in. This textile has both three- and four-ply commercial aniline-dyed yarns. It is also fringed, common in Germantown weavings but extremely rare in other Navajo rugs.

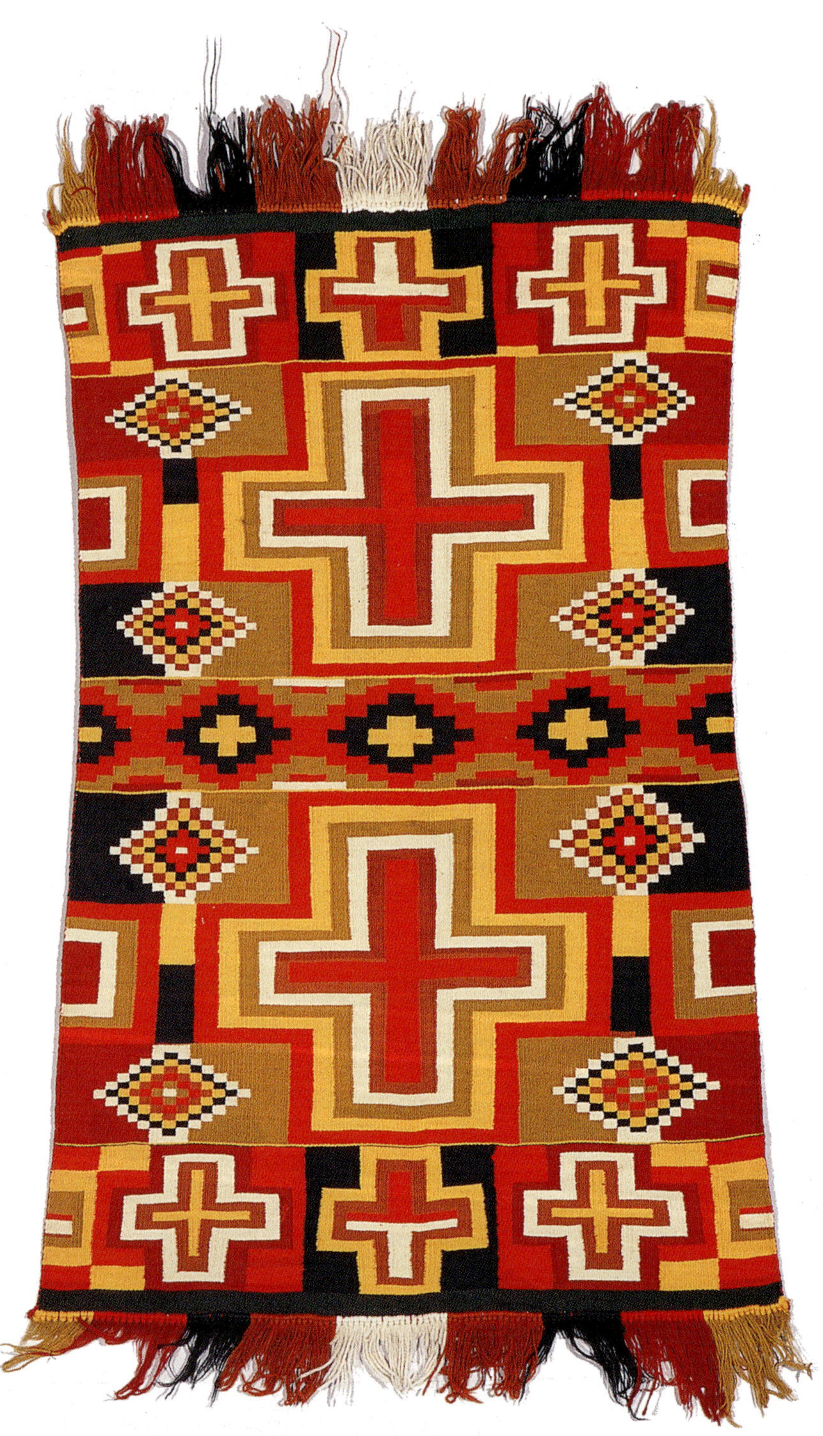

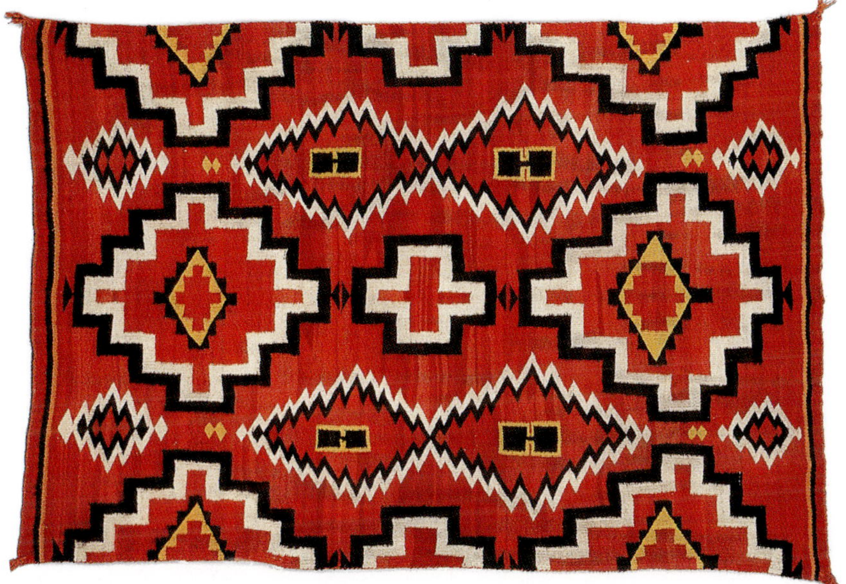

Figure 10. Transitional Period weaving, circa 1890. 78 x 49 in. Handspun aniline-dyed yarns are used in this piece. Note the use of both Classic Period terraced and later serrated-diamond elements with a design strongly reminiscent of chief's blanket patterns.

NAH-doe) Trading Post in Arizona in the late 1870s and refused to buy any rug with a commercial cotton string *warp* (the "skeleton" on which a rug is woven). Weavers had sometimes used cotton instead of handspun wool to save time, but the cotton warps often broke, weakening the structure of the rug. Hubbell also discouraged the use of multiple bright colors, persuading Ganado weavers to produce rugs with natural wool colors and a deep aniline red. He helped weavers return to designs of the Classic Period by having Anglo artists paint examples of the earlier

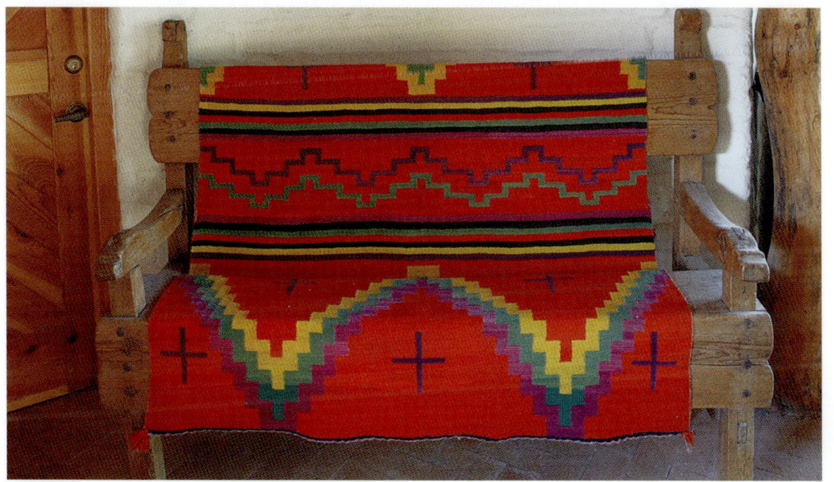

Figure 11. Transitional Period weaving, circa 1880. Handspun aniline-dyed yarn with indigo-dyed yarn end stripes. This near pristine piece shows the incredible vividness of the colors used at the time.

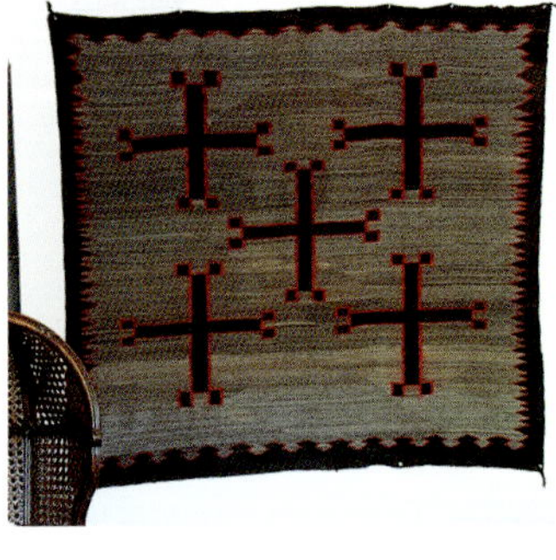

Figure 12. Ganado weaving, circa 1900, with five Spider Woman crosses.

blankets and then hanging them in his post for the weavers to use as guides. Thus Hubbell created some of the first revival weavings, including chief's blanket and wearing blanket styles done as rugs. The weavers also began incorporating old elements like equilateral crosses (later called Hubbell's crosses by many people) or Spider Woman crosses, with two opposing squares at the end of each of the four points. (FIGS. 12 and 13) In the Navajo religion, equilateral crosses represent stars. By 1902, Hubbell was marketing Ganado-area weavings through the Fred Harvey Company, the famous Santa Fe Railroad concessionaire. Since the company shared his appreciation for quality, the demand for improvement in Navajo weaving increased.

John B. Moore of the Crystal Trading Post in New Mexico also instigated new styles of weaving in the mid 1890s. His designs may have been drawn from some traditional sources (see large floor rug on page 6), but many had obvious influences from Oriental rug designs. (FIG. 14) And some were undoubtedly all his own. In addition to introducing new design ideas, Moore also strove to improve the quality of wool used by the Crystal region's artists. At the time, many traders bought and sold rugs by the pound. This, of course, encouraged some weavers not to clean the grease from their wool, thus adding weight. Some even packed sand and dirt into their rugs! The practice gave rise to the notorious "pound blankets." To produce a higher grade of rug, Moore sent wool out to be professionally cleaned before giving it to his better weavers. (However, he did sell some poorer grade rugs by the pound.) Interestingly, Moore was one of the first to produce a mail-order catalog of rug styles for sale in both 1903 and 1911.

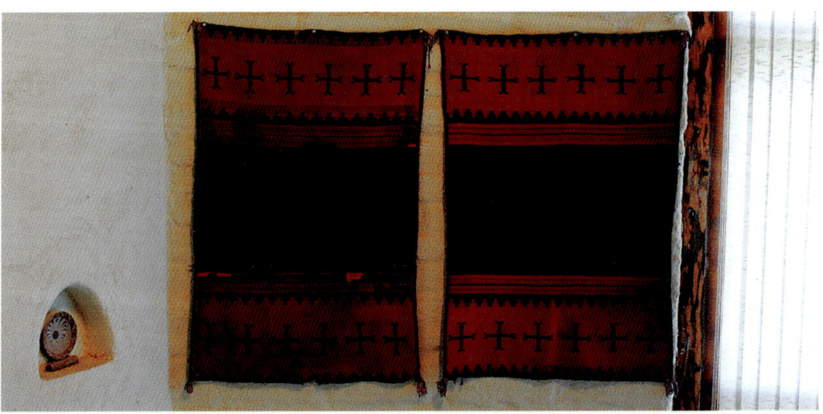

Figure 13. Woman's dress, circa 1865, with raveled cochineal-dyed red and indigo-dyed blue yarns.

By the turn of the twentieth century, the Transitional Period had virtually ended. Blankets disappeared and use of Germantown yarns was also discontinued soon after. Navajo weaving was about to develop a more regional flavor as traders sought to find new markets for rugs.

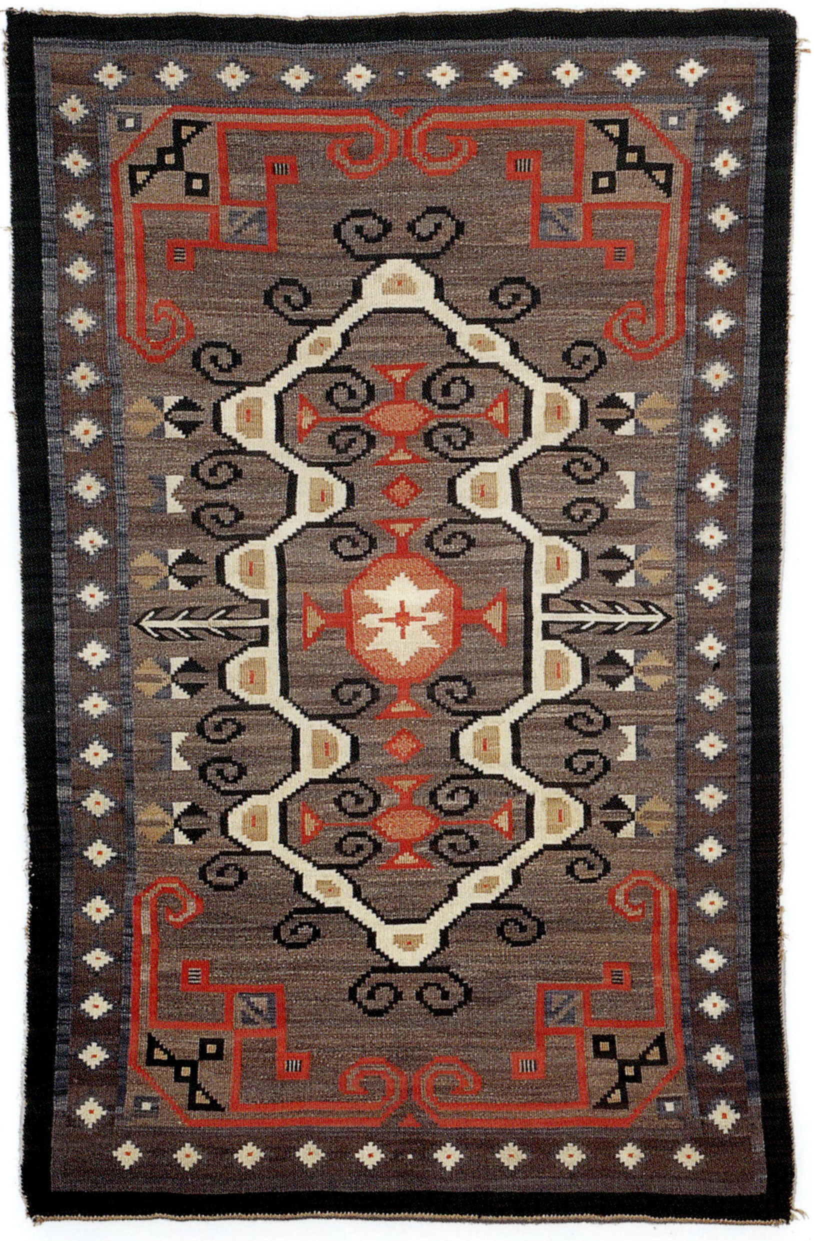

Figure 14. Crystal weaving, circa 1910. 76½ x 50 in. The Oriental rug influence is obvious.

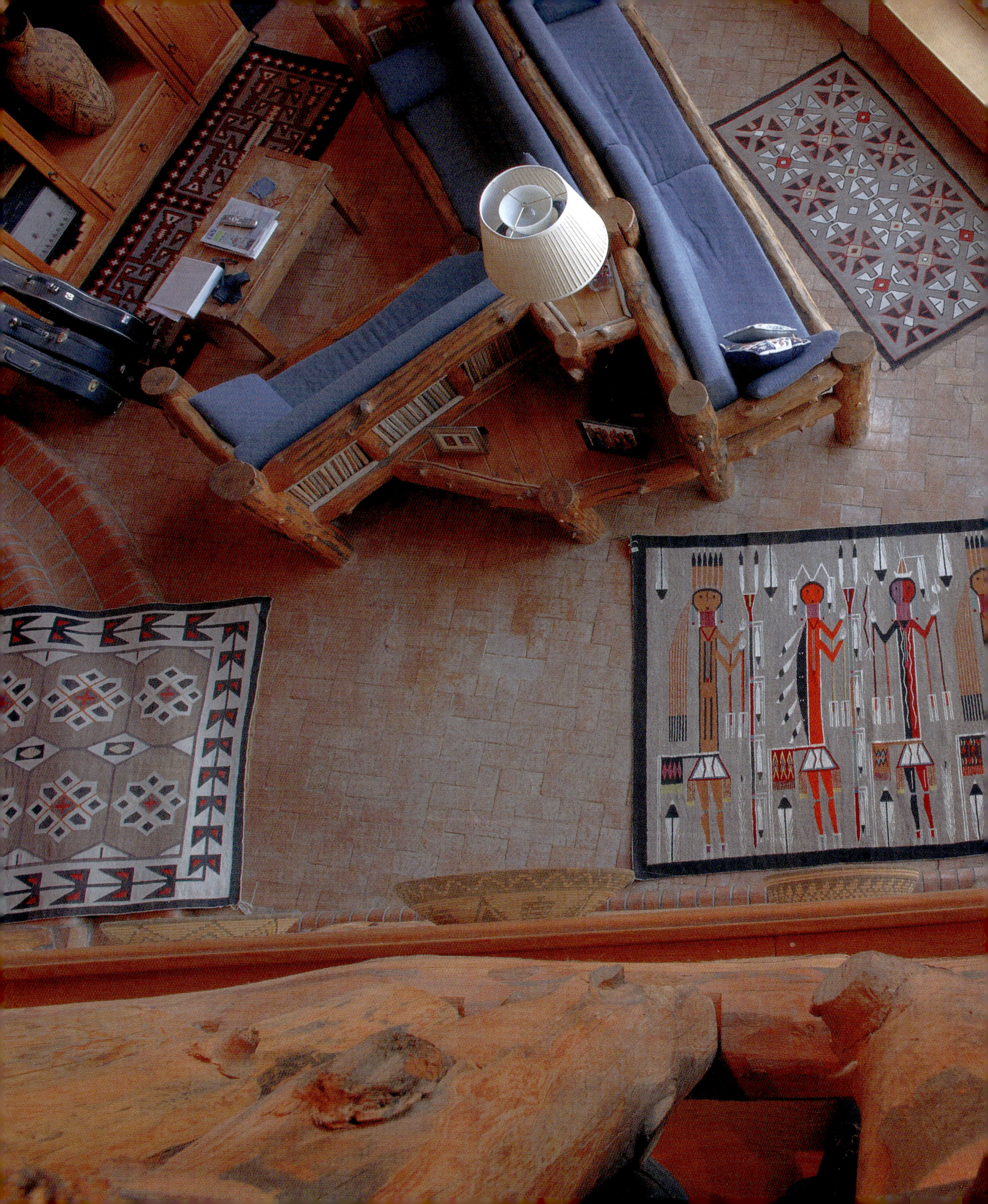

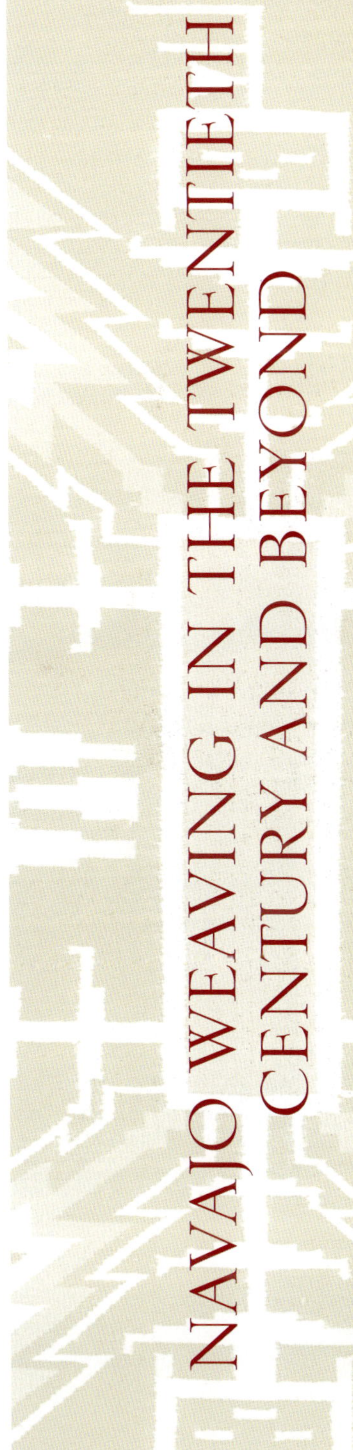

I n this chapter, we will examine both the regional styles and the styles developed by individual weavers in the twentieth and twenty-first centuries and how some of both types came to be. (Unless designated otherwise, all rugs illustrated in this and subsequent chapters were woven after 1990.)

GANADO, TWO GREY HILLS, AND BURNTWATER WEAVINGS

Several regional styles have similar patterns, although their color schemes are different. An obvious starting point must be Ganado and the legacy of Juan Lorenzo Hubbell. The deep red background of Ganado's early weavings has continued to the present day, and a "Ganado Red" is still what many people think of as a Navajo rug. In general, the Ganado area design consists of one or two terraced diamonds in the center, with terraced triangles in each corner. The patterns are also bordered. Colors consist of red, grey, white, black, and sometimes shades of brown. Traditionally, the red and black were aniline-dyed, and the other colors were from the natural wool. Today most are woven with commercially dyed yarn. (FIG. 15)

The weavers in the nearby area of Klagetoh produce a style similar to Ganado's but with a predominantly red pattern on a grey background. However, many Ganado rugs have this same color scheme. As contemporary weavers do fancier

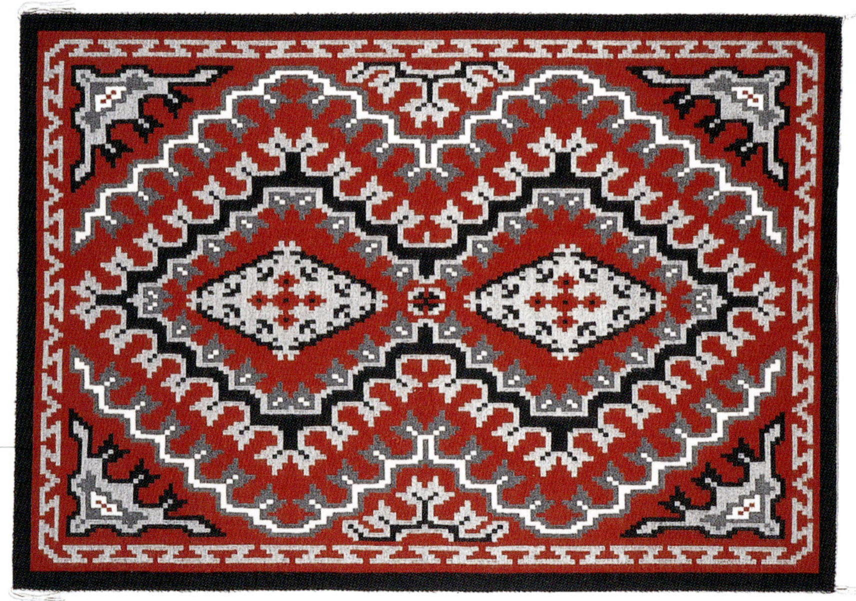

Figure 15. Ganado weaving by Beth Tapaha. 72½ x 49½ in. This exemplifies the deep red background long associated with this area.

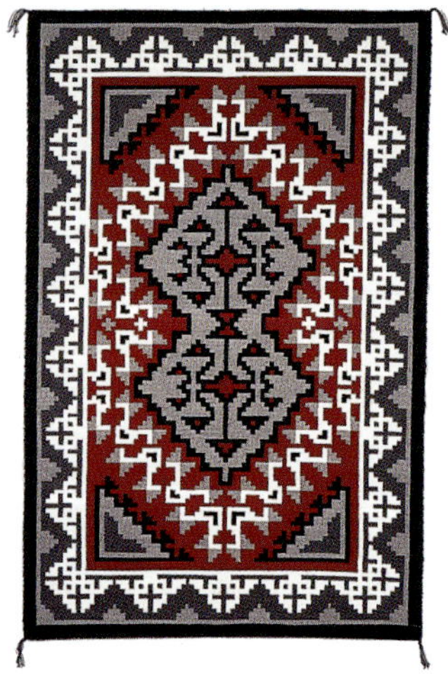

Figure 16. Ganado weaving by Katherine Nez. 70 x 47 in. This is the type of textile referred to as a Klagetoh weaving by many dealers.

multiple borders, the question becomes what is the main pattern and what is the true background? (FIG. 16)

Similar in design but much more subdued in color are the famous Two Grey Hills weavings. Although Two Grey Hills patterns probably had roots in John B. Moore's Crystal rugs, two traders helped develop this specific style. One was Ed Davies, who purchased the Two Grey Hills Trading Post in 1909, and the other was George Bloomfield, who became the resident trader at nearby Toadlena (tode-LEE-nah) at about the same time. Both worked diligently with their area's weavers to develop better weavings. By the mid 1920s, the Two Grey Hills style was well established. The weavers preferred the browns, greys, and whites of natural sheep wool along with a dyed aniline black, rather than the red of Ganado weavers. The overall patterns originally had stacked design elements but over the years became one or two terraced diamonds with terraced corner triangles in a bordered rug. Today, backgrounds are either grey, white, or shades of brown. (FIG. 17)

Burntwater weavings are an additional type using bordered patterns with central terraced diamonds. Unlike the others, they comprise a relatively new style. Weaver Philomena Yazzie is credited with creating the first such rug in 1968, using vegetal-dyed colors (plant sources for the dyes). Burntwater trader Don Jacobs

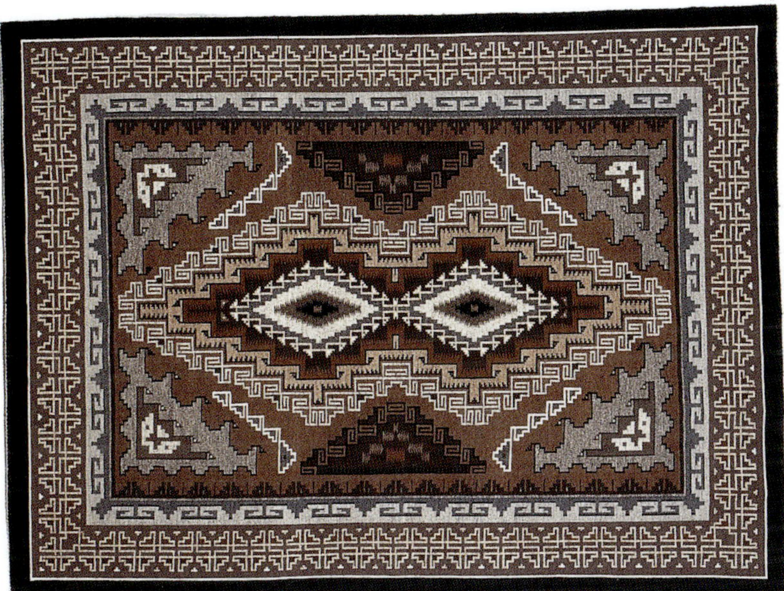

Figure 17. Two Grey Hills weaving by Rita Bedah. 72½ x 53 in. The intricacy of the pattern shows a level of difficulty unusual even for this area.

encouraged this innovation, and the *Arizona Highways* rug issue of July 1974 made it famous. Early Burntwater weavings had fewer colors (perhaps eight to ten) and less intricate patterns than they do today. By the mid 1980s, Bruce Burnham of Sanders, Arizona, was encouraging weavers in the area to include as many as forty

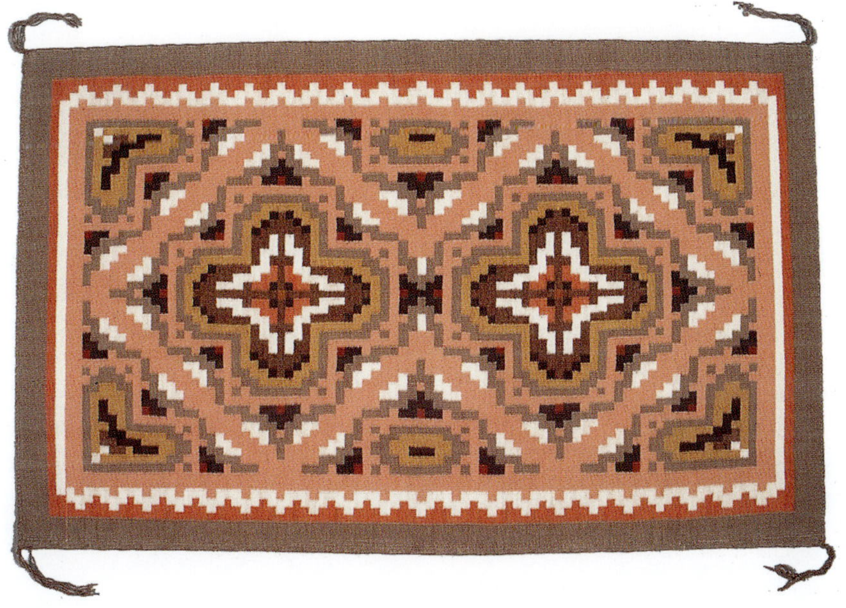

Figure 18. Burntwater tapestry by Barbara Teller Ornelas, circa 1990. 30 x 18½ in. This amazing tapestry has, on average, 92 wefts per inch as well as an elaborate design.

colors per rug. Some Burntwater-style weavers still use vegetal-dyed wool, but many have gone over to commercially dyed yarns. (FIG. 18)

Indeed, considering the available array of pre-dyed yarns as well as packaged dyes and colors derived from many other sources, it is often difficult, to say the least, to determine the actual origin of many colors used in such weavings.

At one point in the early 1980s, we had noticed an unusual number of pieces containing pale and medium blue dyes, purportedly from vegetal sources. We asked a famous weaver from the Crystal area, who had been a trusted friend for a number of years, about her belief regarding the truth of these stories. She began a lengthy and animated tale, explaining that one must go at just the right time of year to seek out the flowers of blue penstemon and blue lupine on mesa tops above 5,000 feet in elevation. Once a sufficient quantity has been gathered, she said, one

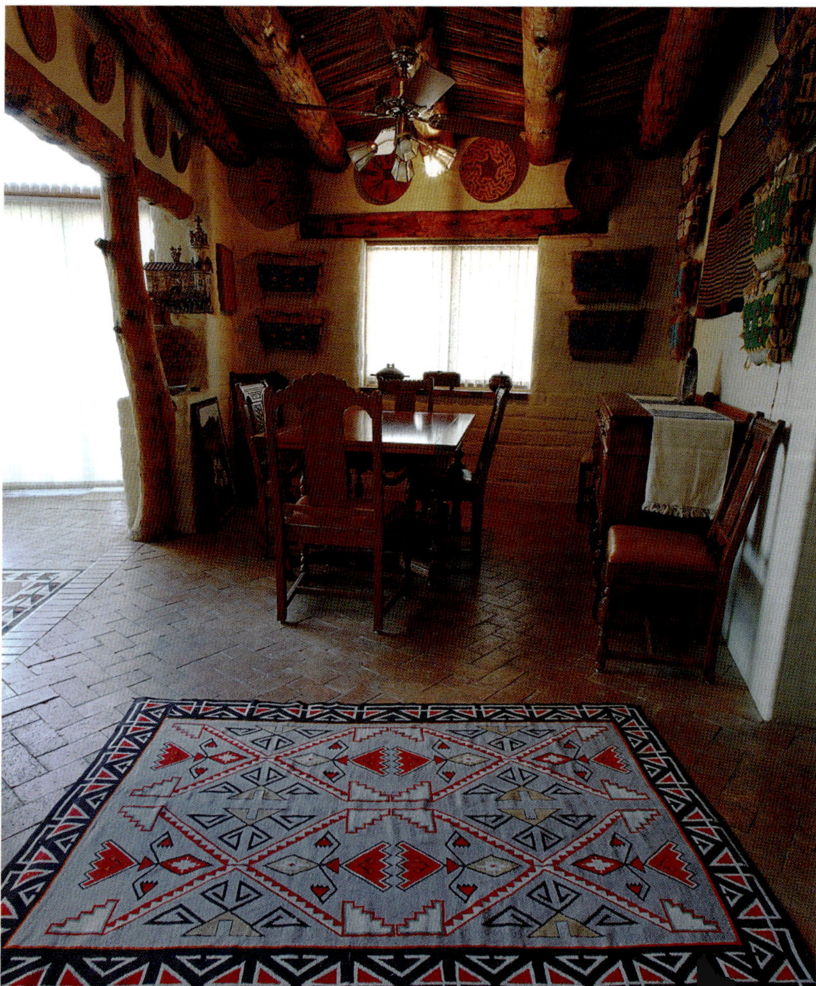

Figure 19. Teec Nos Pos weaving, circa 1930, with handspun yarn.

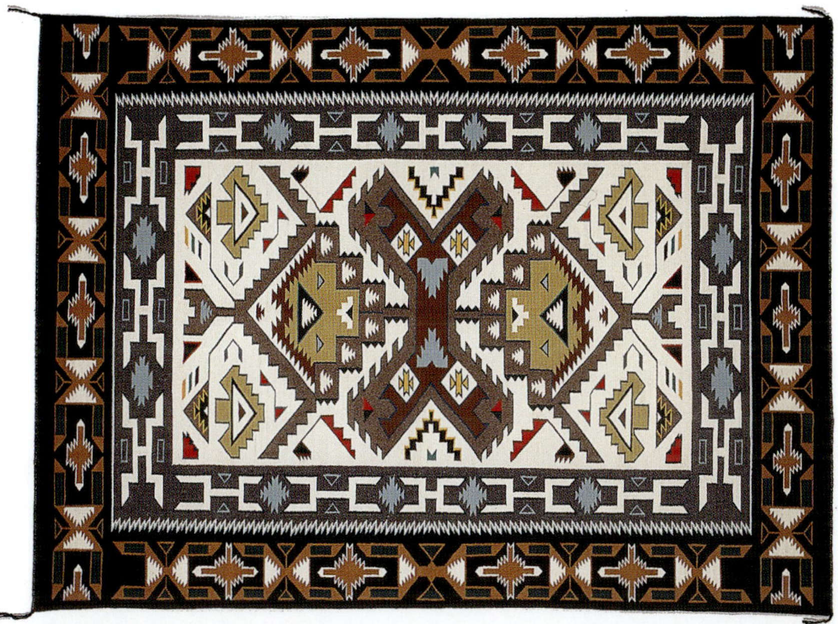

Figure 20. Teec Nos Pos weaving by Pearl Ben. 81½ x 59 in. Note the multiple colors, figured double borders, and complex pattern associated with Teec Nos Pos textiles.

must simmer this material slowly and gently for some length of time. Then, with a twinkle in her eye, she added, "while the flowers cook, you go down to the trading post, get a pack of blue dye, dump it in the pot, and it's done!"

OTHER BORDERED STYLES

Two styles of Navajo weaving have evolved in the Four Corners area: Teec Nos Pos (TEES-nahs-PAHS) and Red Mesa. Around 1900, designs influenced by those of Oriental rugs became synonymous with Teec Nos Pos weavings. Hambleton Bridger Noel, the region's trader at the time, took no credit for the development. Some claim a missionary developed the ideas, and some believe the motifs were derived from some of John B. Moore's Crystal rugs. Elaborately figured borders, double-cross patterns, Xs, and hooked figures in a wide range of bright colors are their trademarks. Weavers also now produce somewhat less busy designs and more subtle colors to keep up with a changing rug market. Before World War II, most Teec Nos Pos rugs were woven with handspun yarn. (FIG. 19) Afterwards, commercial yarn became prominent. (FIG. 20)

Red Mesa outline rugs, as they are often called, are clearly derived from the eye-dazzler textiles of the Transitional Period. They have multiple, stacked, serrated diamonds outlined in different colors, sometimes with borders containing figured elements. Some people do not consider Red Mesa as a separate type from Teec Nos Pos, even though their origins are clearly different. (FIG. 21)

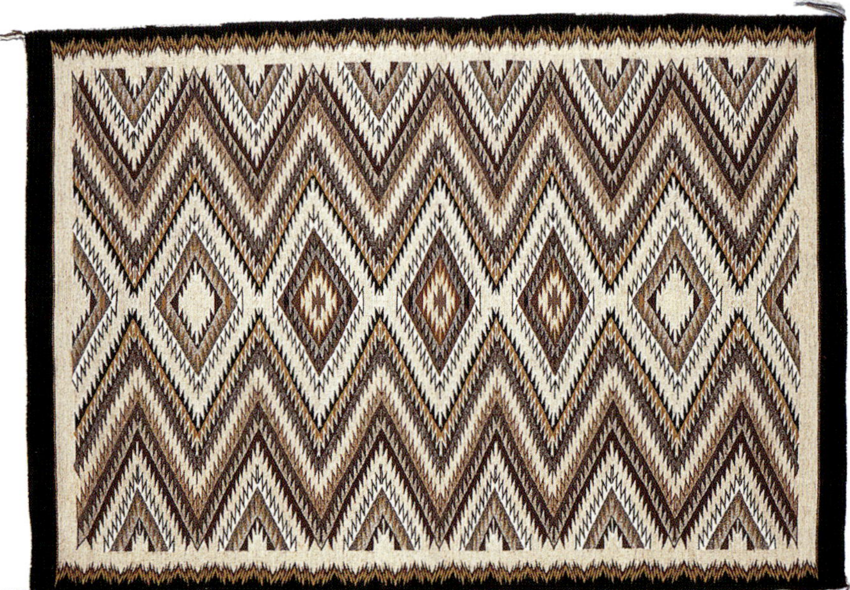

Figure 21. Red Mesa outline weaving by Jason Harvey, 53 x 36 in. The "eye-dazzler" effect is muted by the softer colors.

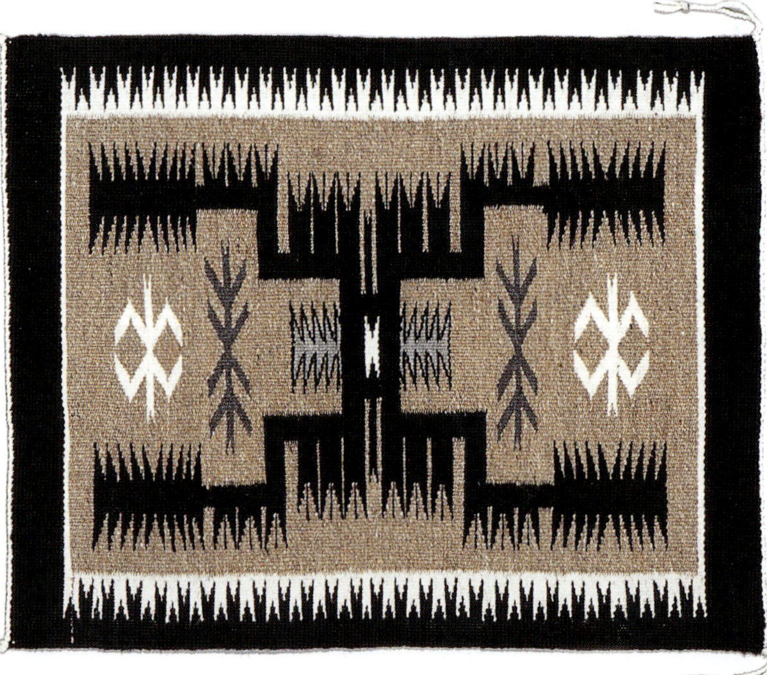

Figure 22. Storm pattern weaving by Elsie Whitehorse. 24 x 19 in. This shows the classic storm pattern in its most basic form.

The storm pattern rug is another bordered design that may have developed in the fertile mind of Moore. Such a rug appeared in his 1911 catalog, in which he claimed its connection to Navajo mythology. Alternatively, the pattern's source may lie in a logo on the tags of flour-sacks sold on the reservation. Some have attributed it to a trader around 1900 at Red Lake Trading Post in the Western Reservation. For many years, the Western Reservation area produced most of the storm pattern rugs. Many stories about the "symbolic" and "religious" meanings of the storm pattern have been told. Whether any of them reflect true Navajo beliefs is questionable. (FIG. 22)

THE BANDED STYLES

Horizontally banded patterns developed in three regions. The first was in Chinle (CHIN-leh) at the mouth of Canyon de Chelly (duh SHAY). In the early 1920s, trader L. H. "Cozy" McSparron, with the help of patron Mary Cabot Wheelwright, sought a return to the old Classic Period of banded styles without borders. This began another revival cycle in Navajo weaving. McSparron and Wheelwright also prompted experimentation with plant dyes. While Navajo weavers had used vegetal dyes as far back as the early nineteenth century, there were never more than

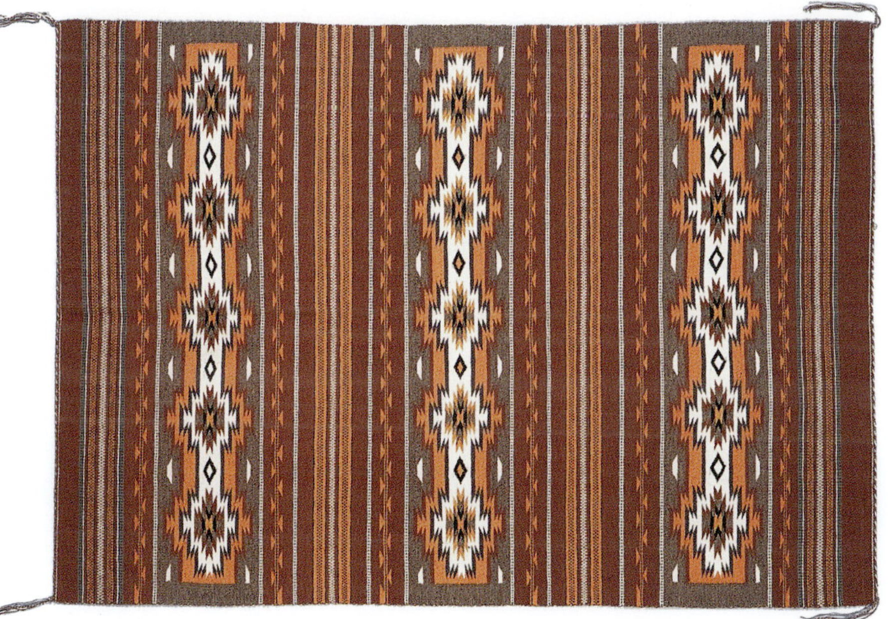

Figure 23. Wide Ruins weaving by Peggy Lynch. 52½ x 36½ in. Atypically, the serrated banded patterns do not extend to the edges of this rug.

Figure 24. Crystal weaving by Lydia Peshlakai. 57 x 47 in. Note the wavy line panels versus the "bead stitch" elements of the Wide Ruins textile.

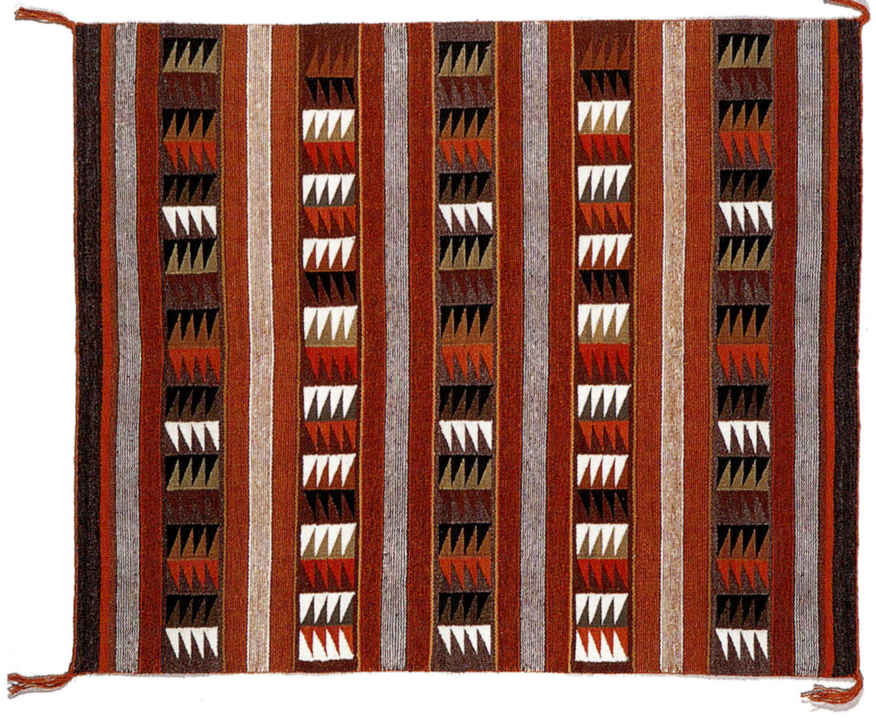

a few (yellow, green, and reddish brown) in common usage by the twentieth century. In 1940, Nonabah Bryan, a Navajo weaving teacher, wrote a pamphlet on how to create eighty-four plant dyes. Chinle weavings continue in the banded style in earth-tone colors, but their identification by pattern has become difficult at best, as they share many characteristics with Wide Ruins and Crystal textiles.

After purchasing the Wide Ruins Trading Post in 1938 and seeing the success of Chinle rugs, William and Sallie Lippincott also encouraged area weavers in the banded style. Of utmost importance to the Lippincotts was quality. Wide Ruins rugs incorporated more colors and intricate designs than those from Chinle. (FIG. 23) They featured a bead stitch of alternating *weft* colors, sometimes referred to as "railroad tracks," in some of the bands. (The weft is the succession of visible threads going across the face of the weaving.) Nearby Pine Springs weavers produce a very similar style but usually include a fair amount of green in the pattern. Many people do not recognize Pine Springs as a regional style.

J. B. Moore's Crystal Trading Post went through several traders after he left in 1911. The old style of Crystal rug with its elaborately figured designs disappeared over time. In 1944, Don Jensen took over the post and promoted banded pattern

Figure 25 (opposite). Indian Chief's pictorial runner, circa 1940.

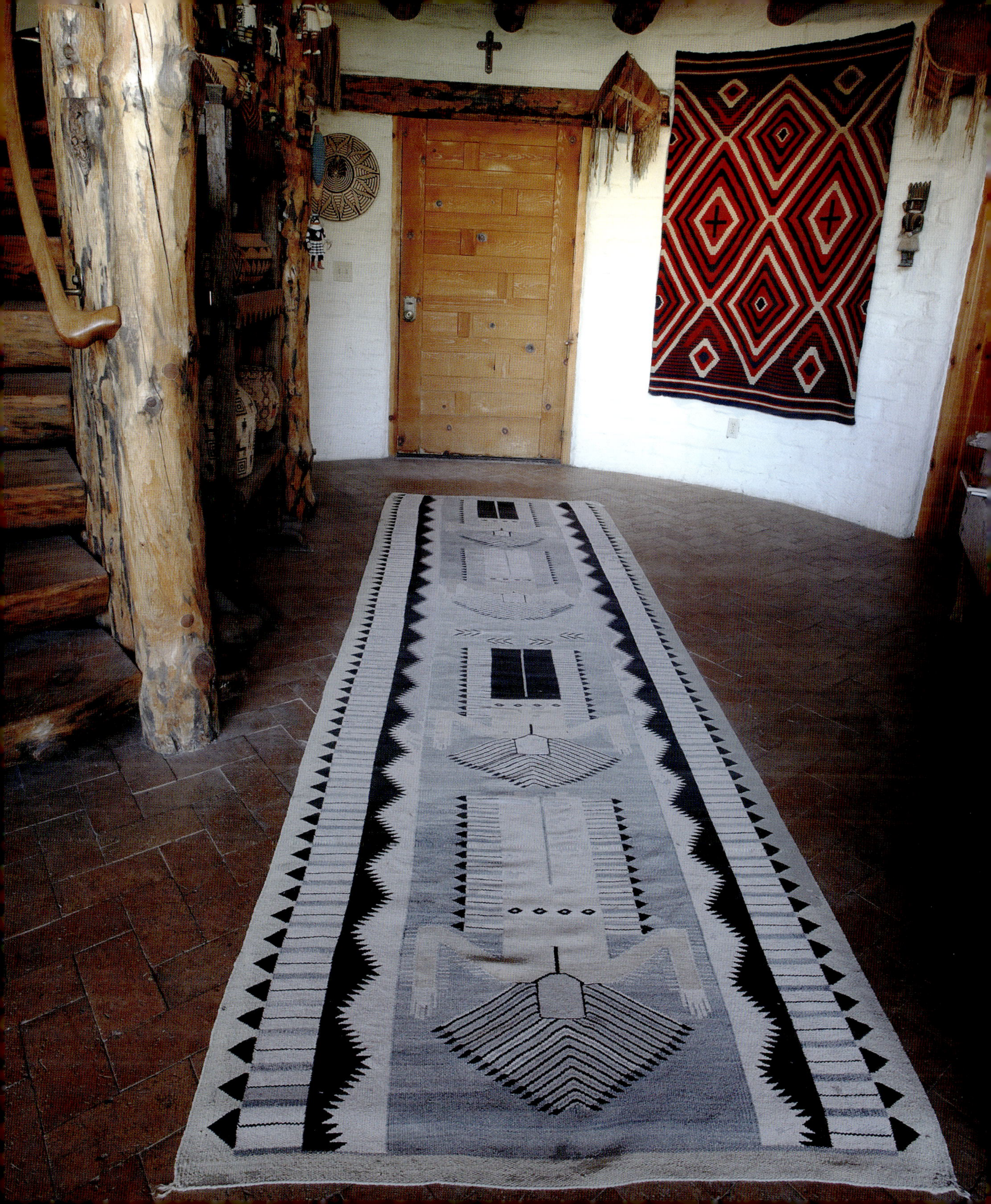

Figure 26. Pictorial weaving, circa 1940. 46 x 46 in. The "floating" bull and cow heads exemplify early pictorial design placement.

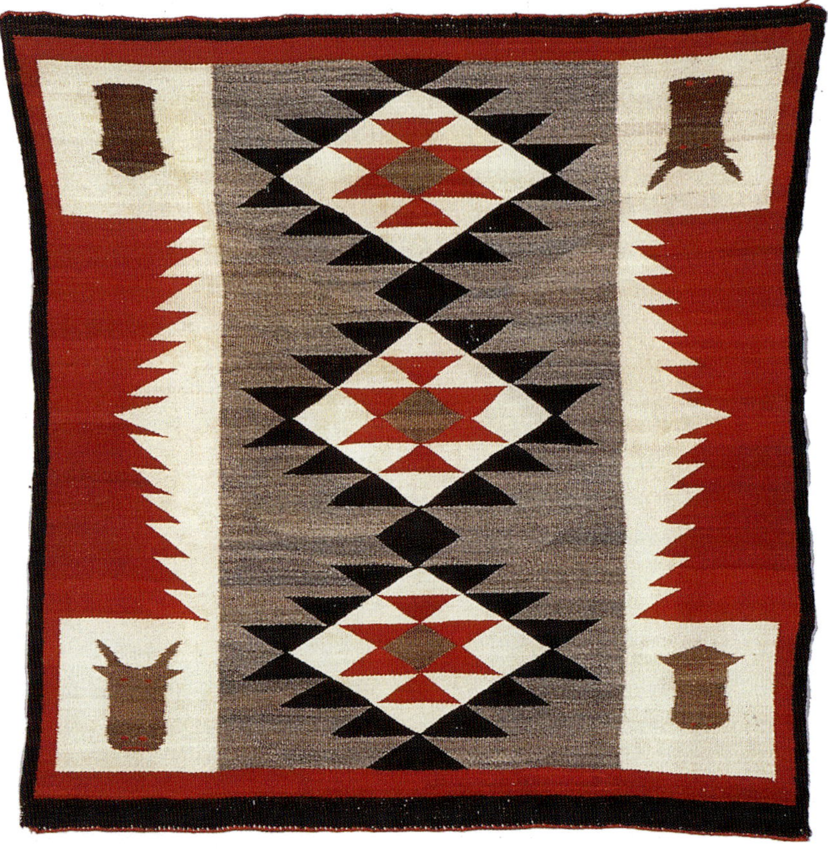

weaving. The area's weavers developed a wavy line effect in most of their banded designs and still use it today. (FIG. 24)

PICTORIAL WEAVINGS

A wide variety exists in pictorial weavings. Many developed through experimentation, while others are rooted in Navajo religion. The real impetus behind their evolution has long been the trader.

Weavings with pictorial elements may have first appeared as early as the 1840s. Four small birds can be seen on a wearing blanket owned by the Cheyenne chief White Antelope when he was killed at the Sand Creek Massacre in 1864. A photograph dated to 1873 shows a Navajo weaver with a United States flag-design rug she had made. By the 1880s and 90s, textiles with trains, animals, people, and letters from the alphabet started to appear. At first these were usually only floating design elements. (FIGS. 25 and 26) But soon the pictorial pattern became the main focus of the weaving, and some featured fully developed scenes.

Yé'ii (YEH-ee) figures appeared on rugs before the turn of the twentieth century. (A Yé'ii is a powerful Navajo supernatural being.) At first, the Navajo considered putting a Yé'ii into a rug design taboo. Near the turn of the century Navajo weaver Yanapah, married to Richard Simpson (a trader near Farmington, New Mexico), wove large, single- and double-figure, vertical Yé'ii rugs. (The figures were standing upright as the rug was being woven.) Today, traders Steve and Georgianna Kennedy Simpson of Bluff, Utah (no relation to Richard Simpson), are trying to revive this style of Yé'ii rug. The first "Simpson Yé'ii" revival was woven in 1995 by Anita Hatathle. (FIG. 27)

Yé'ii rugs developed in two other regions a few years after 1900. At Shiprock, New Mexico, trader Will Evans helped develop multiple-figure Yé'ii weavings in the 1920s. They usually had white or light-colored backgrounds with several figures positioned horizontally across the rug as it was being woven. (The figures stood upright when the rug was turned sideways after weaving.) They had a multitude of bright, aniline-dyed colors and frequently used a great deal of commercial yarn. In the Lukachukai (LOO-kah-CHEW-kye) area, a similar horizontal Yé'ii rug developed but was generally larger and somewhat coarser from the use of handspun yarn. They usually had darker backgrounds and more subdued colors. Today there is virtually no

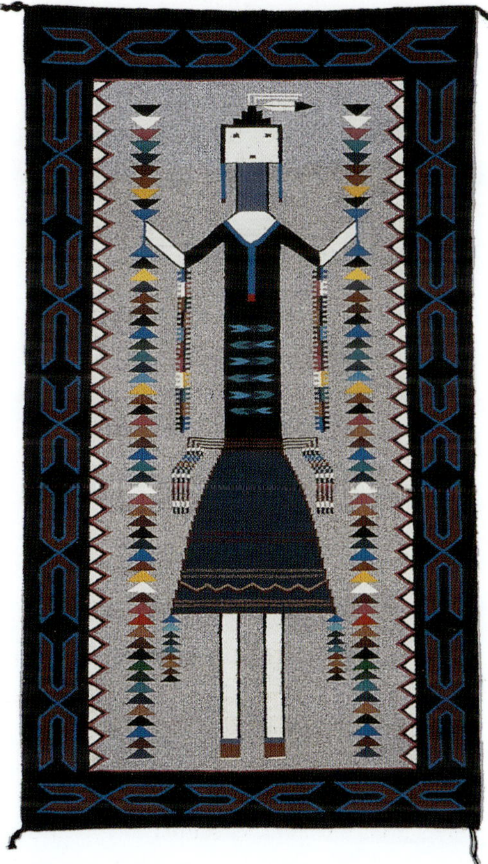

Figure 27. Simpson Yé'ii revival weaving by Marjorie Dee. 60 x 34 in. Note the vertical layout of the textile as opposed to the horizontal layout of the rug in Figure 28.

distinction as to which region a Yé'ii rug comes from. Many kinds of new border treatments and colors are prevalent. Yé'ii weavings often have a rainbow Yé'ii or guardian surrounding three sides of the other Yé'ii. (FIG. 28)

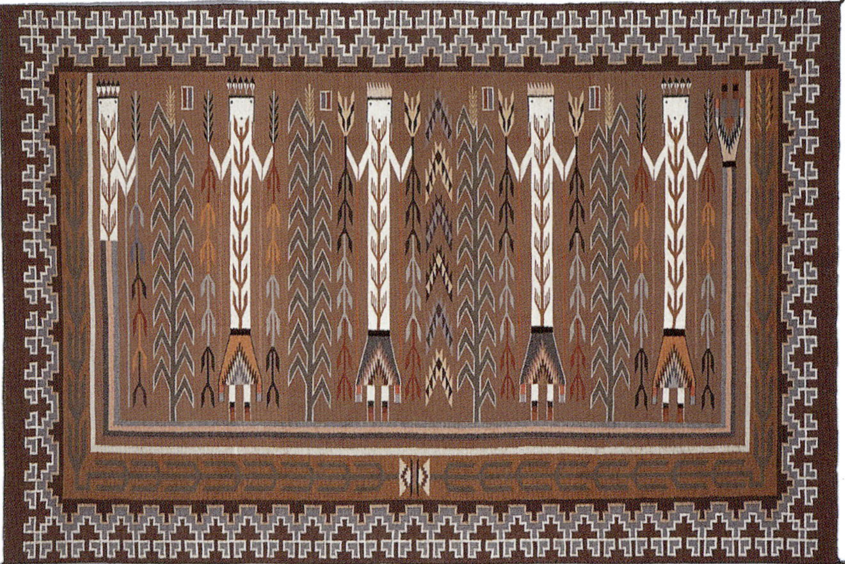

Figure 28. Yé'ii weaving by Rose Yazzie. 71½ x 47½ in. The Rainbow Yé'ii is shown in a U shape around the other Yé'ii.

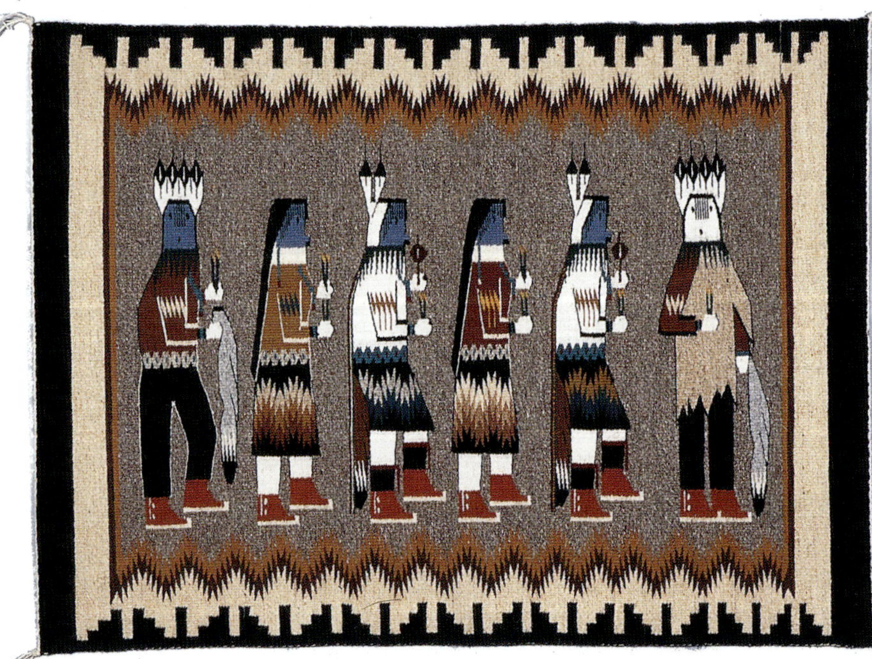

Figure 29. Yé'ii Bicheii weaving by Daisy Nakai. 38 x 27½ in. The white-faced figure at the head of the line is the Yé'ii Bicheii, while the others are Yé'ii.

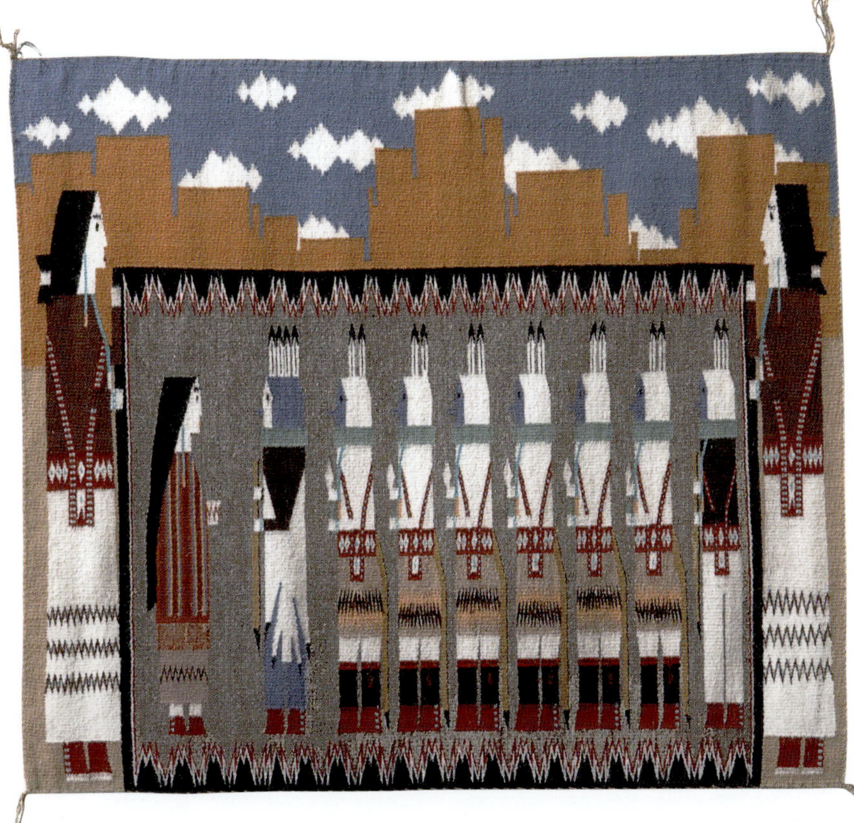

Figure 30. Women holding a pictorial weaving of a Yé'ii Bicheii weaving with an additional pictorial background, by Louise Yazzie. 28 x 24 in. Louise is the daughter of the late Betty Bia, who along with her sister Della Woody Begay, popularized this style of weaving.

An interesting variation of the Yé'ii rug is the Yé'ii Bicheii (YEH-ee bih-SHAY). It was most likely developed in the Shiprock area near the turn of the twentieth century to depict the Nightway ceremony in which Navajo dancers portray Yé'ii Bicheii and other Yé'ii. Yé'ii Bicheii is called Talking God or Grandfather of the Gods. He appears in a white face mask as the lead dancer with other Yé'ii at the winter Night Chant (or Nightway) on the final night of the nine-day curative ceremony. In current vernacular, the term Yé'ii Bicheii is commonly used to describe all weavings in which human masked dancers represent the Yé'ii, regardless of mask color. They are often shown in profile to highlight their distinction from the divine beings. (FIG. 29) A style of Yé'ii Bicheii weaving that developed in the 1970s, this example portrays two women holding a Yé'ii Bicheii rug between them with a pictorial scene behind them (FIG. 30). This is a melding of Yé'ii Bicheii and scenic pictorials as well as an early version of rug-in-a-rug (see page 50).

Figure 31. Sandpainting weaving by Mary Rose Tyler. 52½ x 49 in. This weaving is a version of the Home of the Buffalo sandpainting.

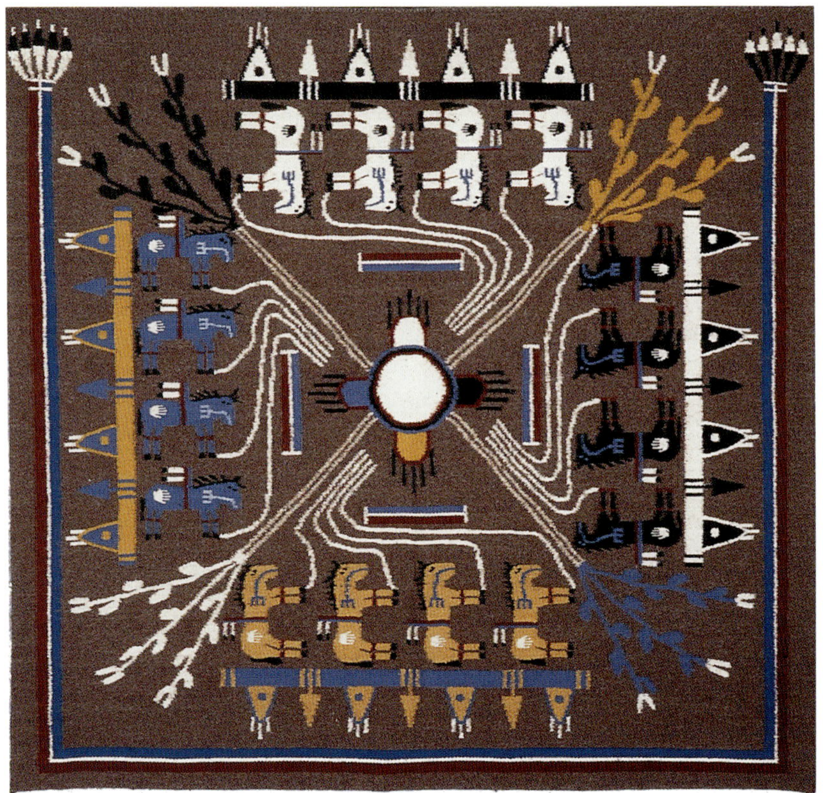

Yé'ii figures also often appear in the famous sandpainting rugs. Ritual sandpaintings, created on the ground by Navajo *hataalii* (ha-TATH-lee), or medicine men, while chanting are at the heart of their religion. There is a multitude of these ceremonial chantways, or "sings" as they are often called, each with its corresponding mythological stories painted in sand to exorcise evil, treat illnesses, confer blessings, and help to restore the world to balance. Because of their sacred nature, it was considered taboo for anyone other than a shaman to recreate them, at the risk of blindness or severe illness. In 1919, Franc Newcomb (the wife of trader Arthur Newcomb of Newcomb, New Mexico) convinced a hataalii named Hosteen Klah (HAHS-teen claw) to weave a sandpainting rug for her. Since he was a medicine man, Hosteen Klah did not have the same prohibition against reproducing it that other weavers had. Klah also convinced his nieces, Gladys and Irene Manuelito, to weave them. Several of their rugs were woven for Mary Cabot Wheelwright and are now housed in the Wheelwright Museum in Santa Fe. A few weavers today still weave sandpainting rugs, often hiring a medicine man to perform a ceremony before or after the rug is woven to ensure protection. Payment for this ceremony adds to the price of an already intricately patterned and, hence, time-consuming and costly weaving. (FIGS. 31 and 32)

Scenic pictorial rugs started to appear in the 1930s. Reservation life is the most common subject today, showing ceremonies or daily activities, depicted in two styles. The older and simpler style is woven in several areas of the reservation and treats the figures in a more naïve, two-dimensional style of representation. Objects are often not shown in perspective regarding size to distance. (FIG. 33) The newer style was started in the 1970s by Linda Nez of Cedar Ridge, Arizona. Several members of the Nez extended family and other weavers now create weavings with a more realistic and defined treatment of the figures. (FIGS. 34 and 35) In addition

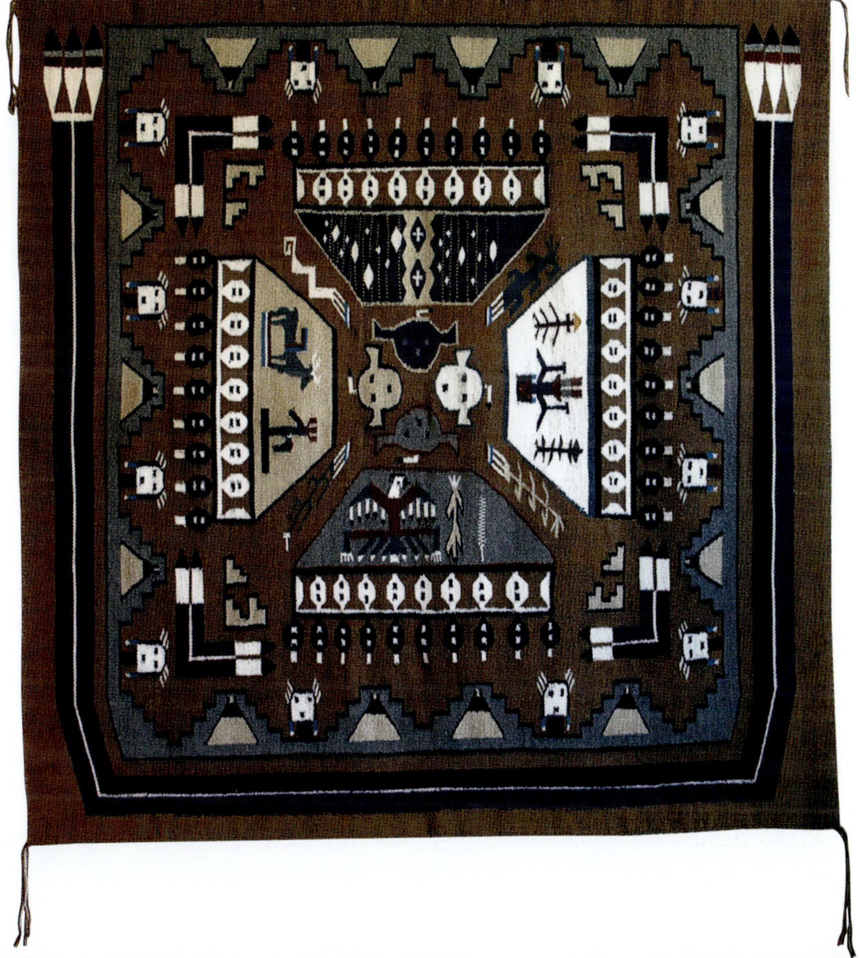

Figure 32. Sandpainting weaving by Zonnie Gilmore. 53½ x 52 in. The weaving depicts a version of the Skies sandpainting from the Male Shootingway chant, with the four sacred plants, sun, moon, and winds. The trapezoidal forms represent the sky at dawn, afternoon, dusk, and night.

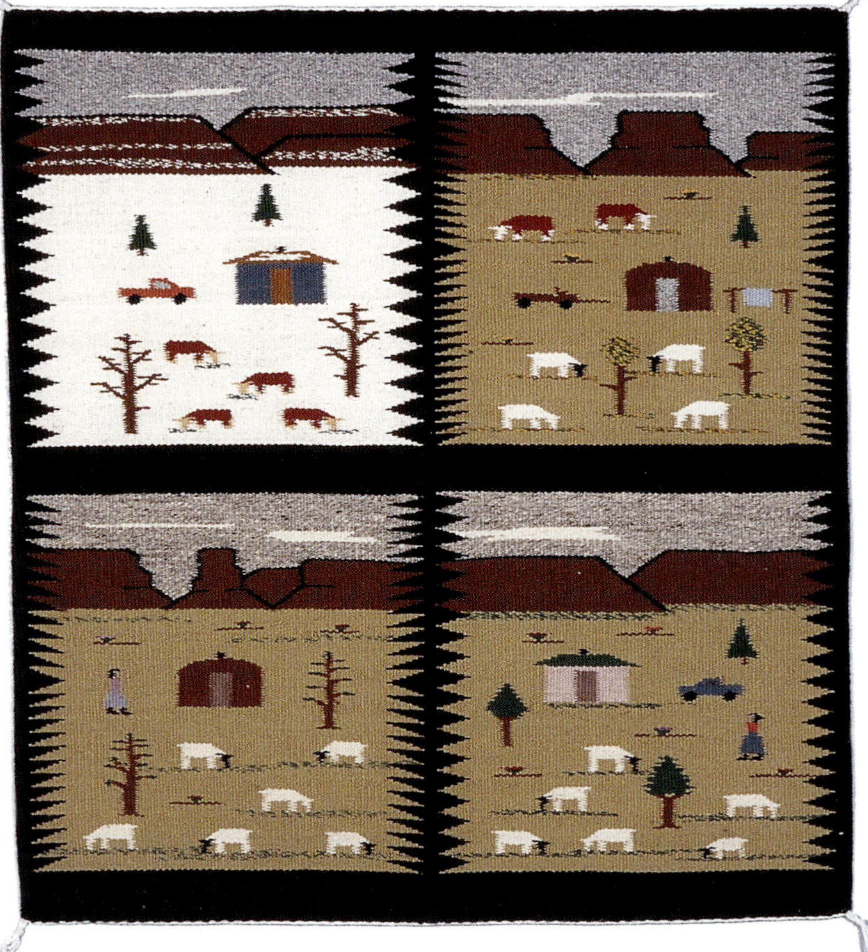

Figure 33. Pictorial weaving by Marie Begay. 27 x 25½ in. The four seasons (clockwise from upper left: winter, spring, summer, and fall) are shown in this older-style reservation scene.

to Navajo subject matter, these weavers also produce pictorials with Plains Indians, dinosaurs, and even Santa Claus. (FIG. 36)

The pattern commonly called the "tree of life," or bird pictorial, first appeared around 1900. Although its provenance is unclear, this pattern may have been derived from certain sandpainting designs. The weavings show birds perched on cornstalks, trees, or generic plants, sometimes with the vegetation growing out of a Navajo wedding basket. (FIG. 37)

A new type of pictorial was created in the Burnham, New Mexico, region in the late 1970s. It was first produced by Helen Begay who, along with her relatives in both the Barber and Begay families, created a most unusual style. It includes many different pictorial elements, such as Yé'ii (FIG. 38) and human figures (FIG. 39), among others, usually mixed in with geometric designs. Burnham-style textiles usually have backgrounds using the Two Grey Hills color palette and are woven in combinations of natural wool, home-dyed, and brighter commercially dyed colors. The geometric patterns themselves may be asymmetrical, an uncommon feature in Navajo weavings. Jackson Clark II of Toh-atin in Durango, Colorado, purchased and promoted most of the early works of Helen Begay and her family. This style seems to have become a permanent part of the Navajo weavers' repertoire.

SPECIAL TECHNIQUES AND SHAPES

Several special weaving techniques make up another group of Navajo textiles. One of the best known is the raised outline weaving. The earliest known example of this

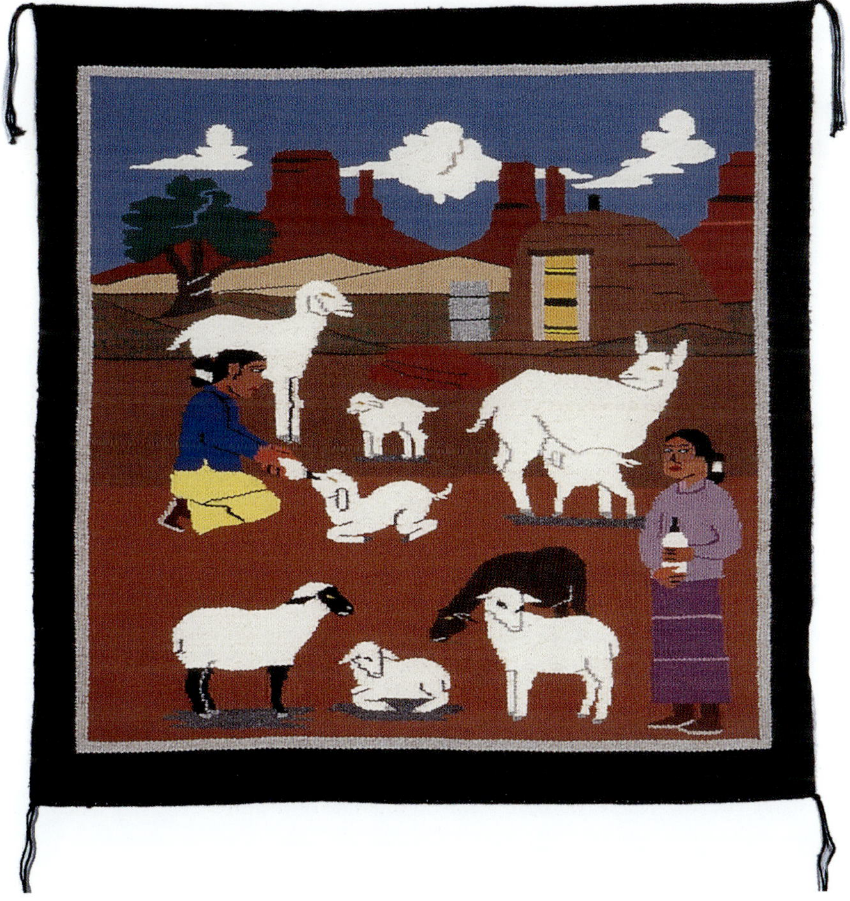

Figure 34. Pictorial weaving by Virginia Nez. 33 x 32½ in. This is the newer style of pictorial weaving, also depicting a scene from reservation life.

Figure 35. Pictorial weaving of an old-style train passing through a pastoral scene with a weaver, by Geanita John. Geanita is the daughter of weaver Isabell John (deceased), who was especially noted for her pictorial weavings portraying Navajo weavers.

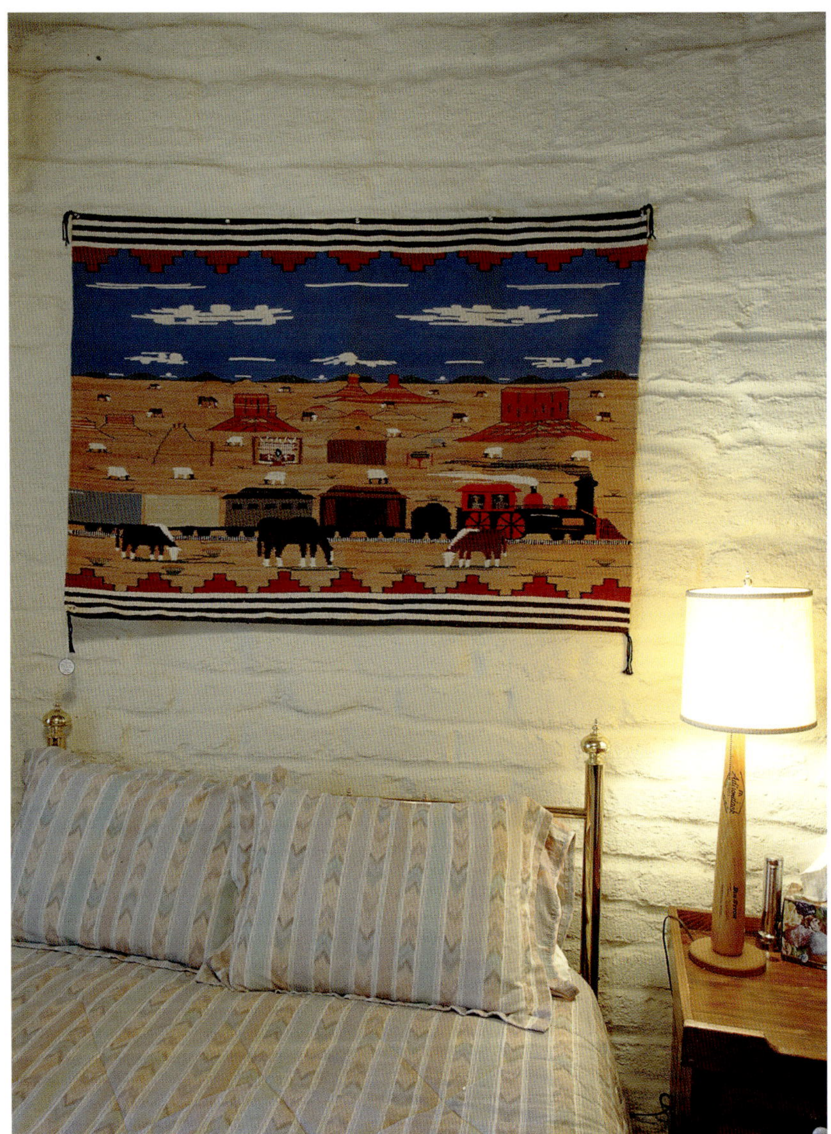

type was woven in the Ganado area in 1934, but the area most associated with this technique is Coal Mine Mesa, Arizona. In 1950, Ned Hatathli helped develop it there through a project of the Navajo Arts and Crafts Guild where he was the manager. In raised outline weaving, all or most of the rug is filled with fine vertical pinstripes of various colors. Raised three-dimensional ridges outline the edges of the design elements. The ridges occur only on one side of the piece, creating a definite front and back. The effect is almost one of viewing the rug through a set of narrow bars and is more impressive with diagonal patterns. Many raised outline weavings are storm pattern rugs produced not only because of their diagonal elements but for their familiarity to Western Reservation weavers as well.

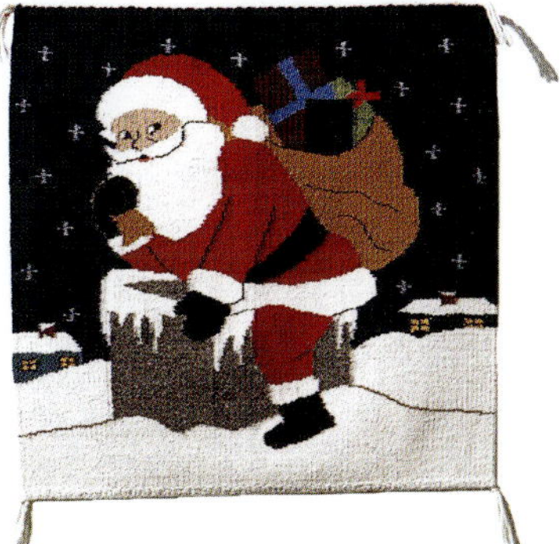

Figure 36. Pictorial weaving of Santa Claus by Tabitha Bitah. 21 x 20 in.

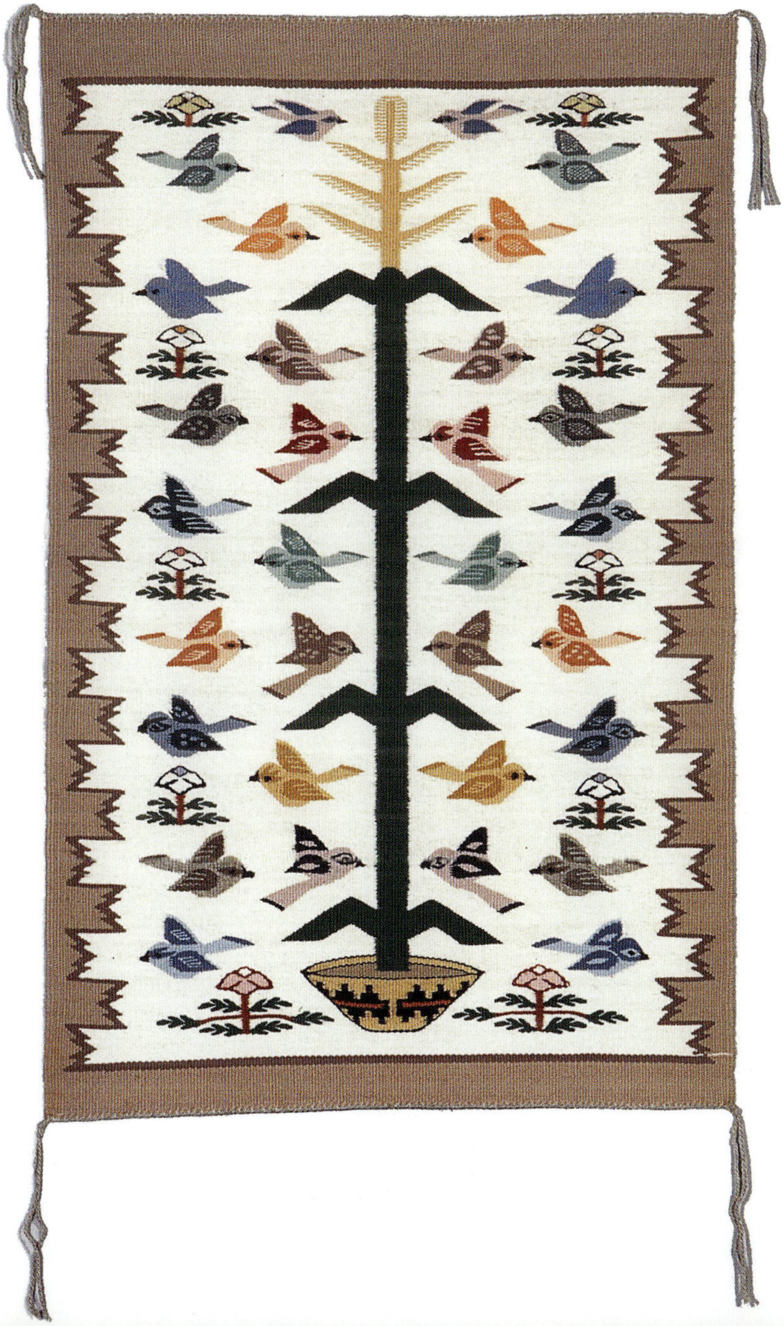

Figure 37. Bird pictorial weaving by Alice Nockideneh. 35 x 23 in. This version has the birds on a cornstalk with the wedding basket at the base.

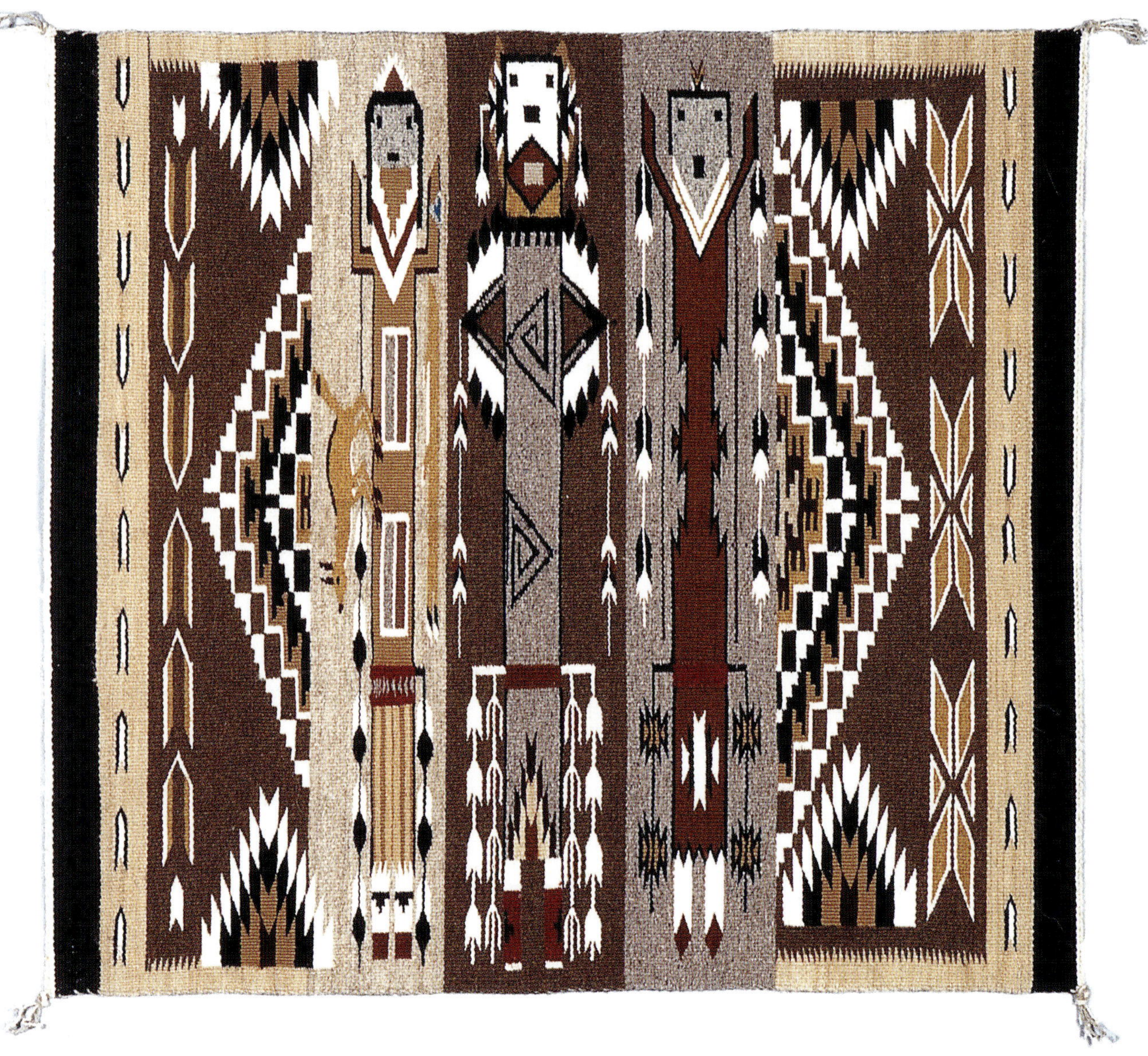

Figure 38. Burnham weaving by Sandra Begay. 30 x 27 in. Note the three different types of Yé'ii as well as the similar but not identical side panels showing Two Grey Hills influence.

In the 1980s, a newer variety of raised outline rug incorporated Teec Nos Pos patterns (fairly diagonal in nature) with soft, vegetal-looking colors (although most are not vegetal-dyed). (FIG. 40) This variety has been called "New Lands" by some, most notably by the trader who helped develop it, Bruce Burnham of Sanders, Arizona. He says Marie Watson Nez, working with trader Bruce McGee (then of Keam's Canyon, Arizona), created the first such weaving. Fortunately for Burnham, many Coal Mine Mesa weavers (including Wanda Begay and her family) were relocated to the New Lands area near Sanders by the mid 1980s. This was a result of the Hopi-Navajo land settlement that moved families (of both tribes) who had been living on the other tribes' territories.

Two-faced weaving is a technique requiring especially patient and talented weavers. It demands an intricate setup of the loom with a minimum of four sheds (as opposed to the normal two), each controlling different combinations of warps. (See the next chapter for a discussion of the Navajo loom.) Two-faced rugs date back to the nineteenth century. Today they are generally a diamond-twill weave surrounding panels of plain weave, bead stitch, or, occasionally, geometric designs on one side and the reverse diamond-twill weave around Yé'ii or geometric-design panels on the other. (FIG. 41)

Diamond- and diagonal-twill weavings also require multiple sheds, three or more. Unfortunately, while both two-faced and twill weavings are technically difficult to accomplish, the prices received for producing them have not increased proportionately compared to other weavings. As buyers look for more variety in pattern, they often ignore these seemingly repetitious but nonetheless highly intri-

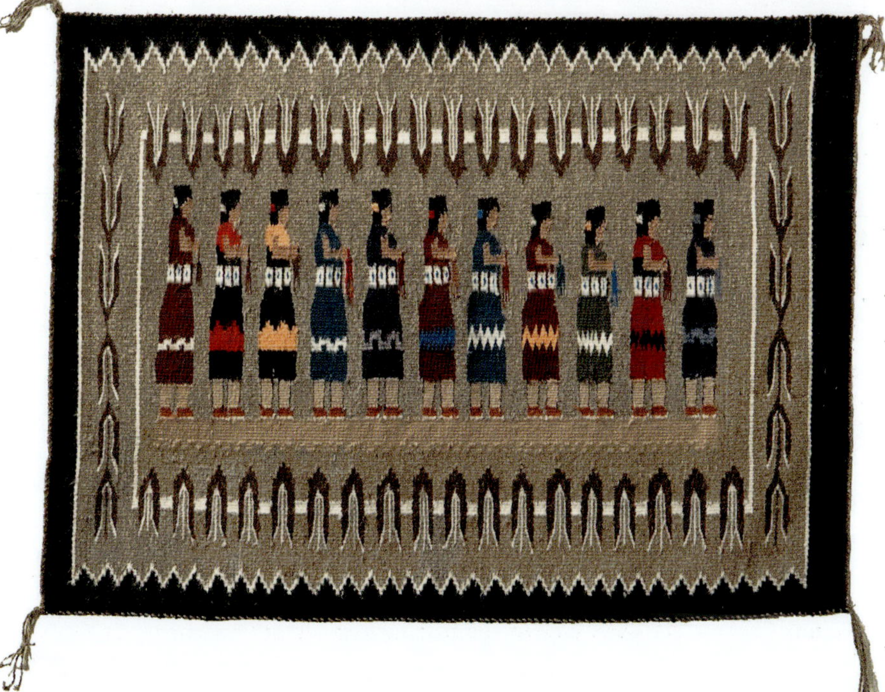

Figure 39. Burnham weaving by Anna Mae Barber. 30½ x 19½ in. The weaving shows a line of Navajo women dancers of varying heights.

cate rugs. Hence, both the two-faced and the diamond- and diagonal-twill types are disappearing.

Tapestry weavings are considered some of the most technically demanding works ever created by Navajo weavers. A tapestry weave is currently defined as 80 wefts (the visible threads going across the face of the weaving) per linear inch, whereas the average Navajo weaving is 25 to 40 wefts per inch. The technique was developed at Two Grey Hills in the 1940s by the late Daisy Tauglechee who was capable of creating tapestries with over 120 wefts to the inch. While they are now produced in other regions, most of the finest still come from Two Grey Hills. (FIGS. 5 and 18)

Innovative Navajo weavers occasionally weave round rugs and cross- or star-shaped styles of rugs. Rose Owens is generally recognized as the round rug creator.

Figure 40. Raised outline weaving by Marietta Blackrock. 51 x 35½ in. This is a very clear example of an intricate Teec Nos Pos pattern using the raised outline technique.

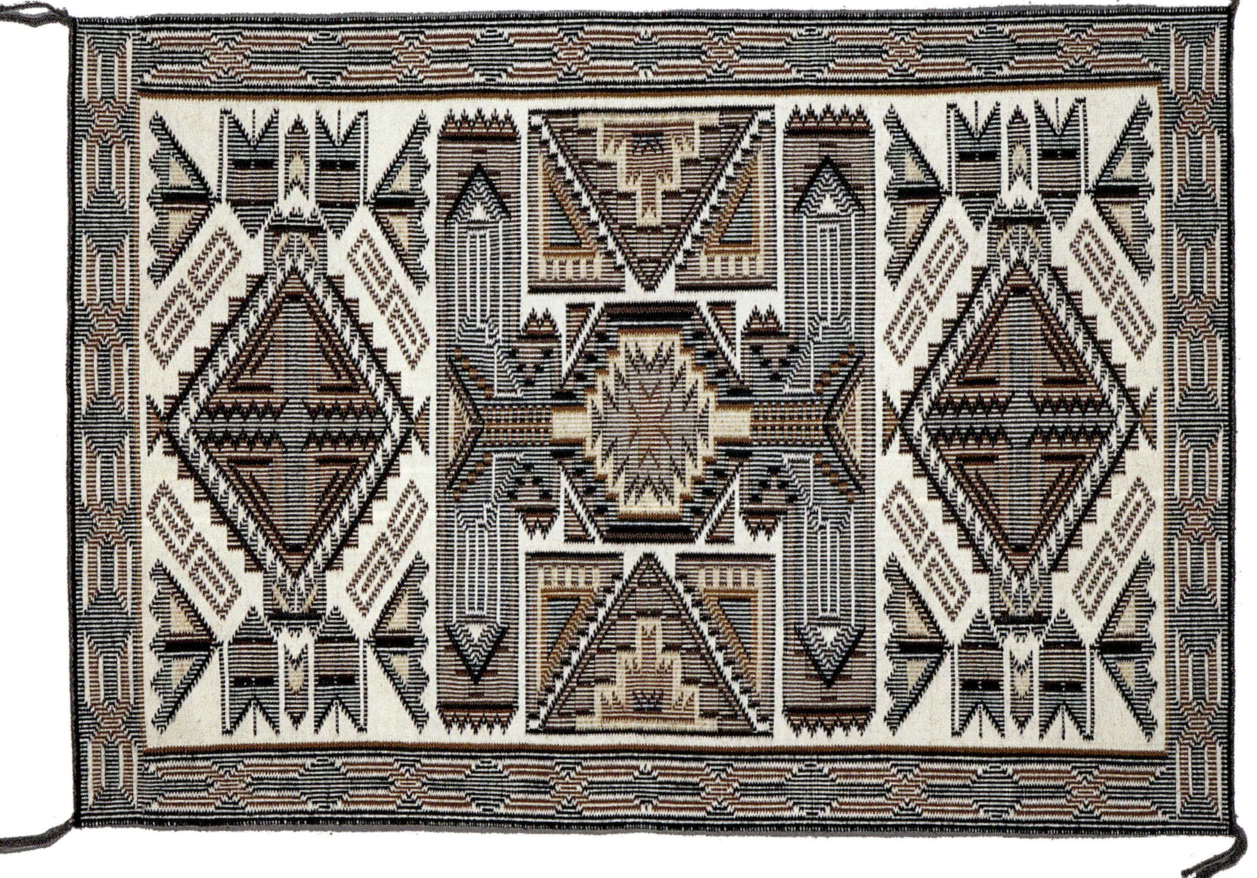

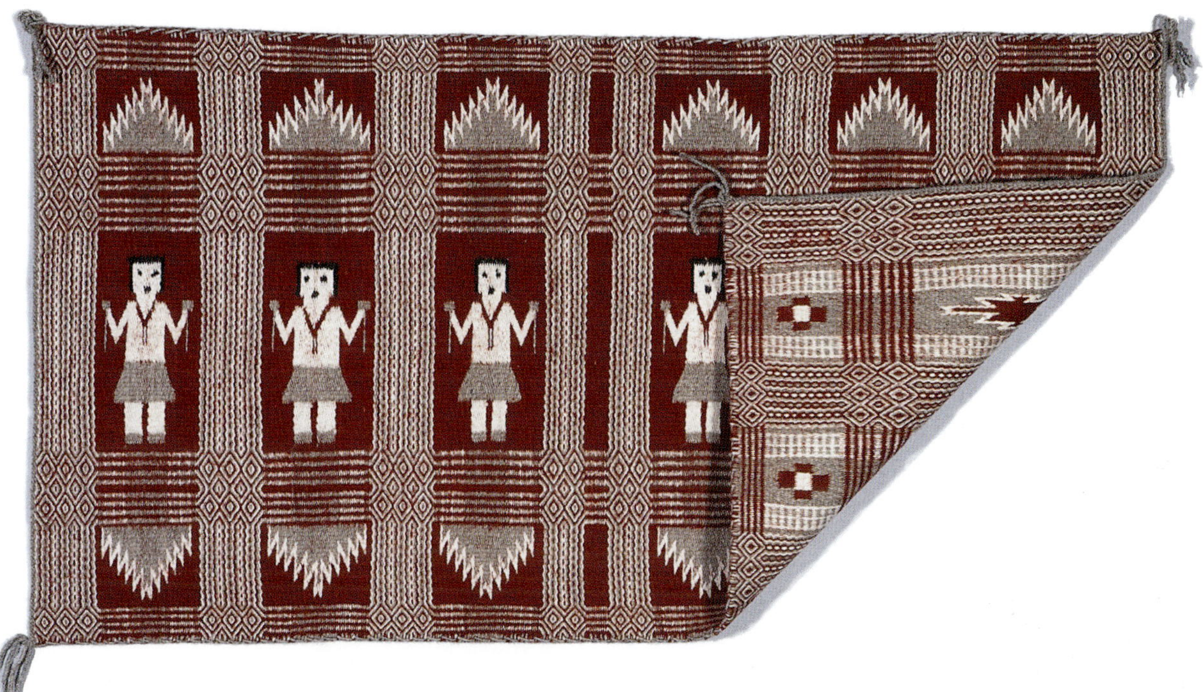

In the late 1960s, she dreamed about Spider Woman (who the Navajos believe taught them to weave) weaving in a circle. Owens's husband brought her the metal rim of a wagon wheel to create the round shape. (FIG. 42) It is unknown when cross-shaped rugs first appeared, but they certainly existed by the mid-twentieth century. (FIG. 43) Weavers of both shapes usually will not divulge their secrets, for fear of being copied.

Miniature weavings also constitute an interesting segment of the Navajo rug market and some collectors specialize in these little gems. True miniatures are woven on small versions of Navajo looms, and their weavers take no shortcuts. Some weavers produce pieces which resemble Navajo weavings but are made on looms other than the

Figure 41. Two-faced weaving by Harriet Snyder. 44½ x 23½ in. The red background behind the Yé'ii and the geometric designs on the front panels contrast particularly well with the grey background of the geometric patterns on the back panels.

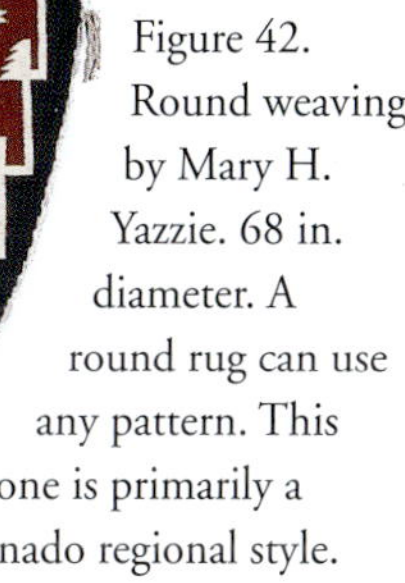

Figure 42. Round weaving by Mary H. Yazzie. 68 in. diameter. A round rug can use any pattern. This one is primarily a Ganado regional style.

Figure 43. Cross- or star-shaped weaving by Alice Begay, circa 1985. 48½ x 47 in. The initial set-up of the loom creates this unique shape.

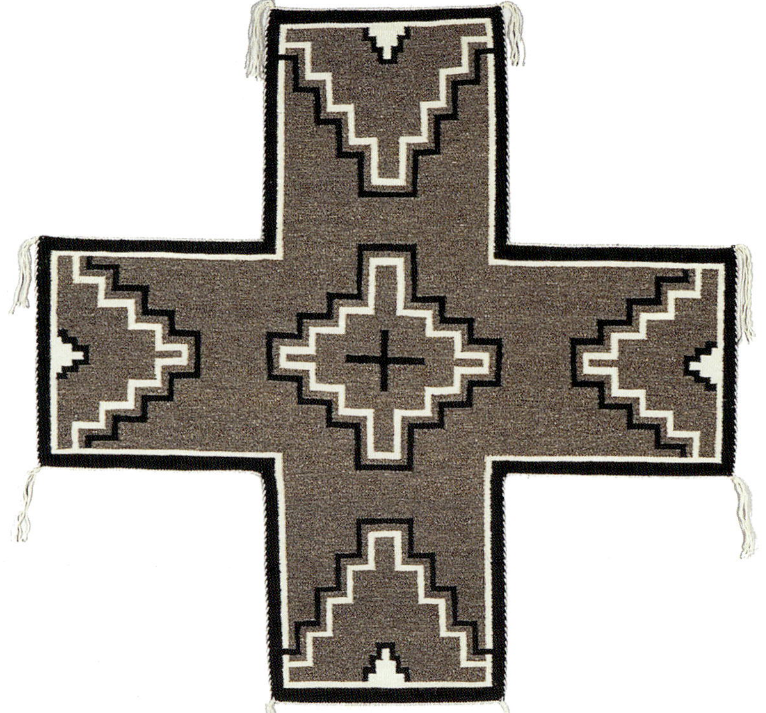

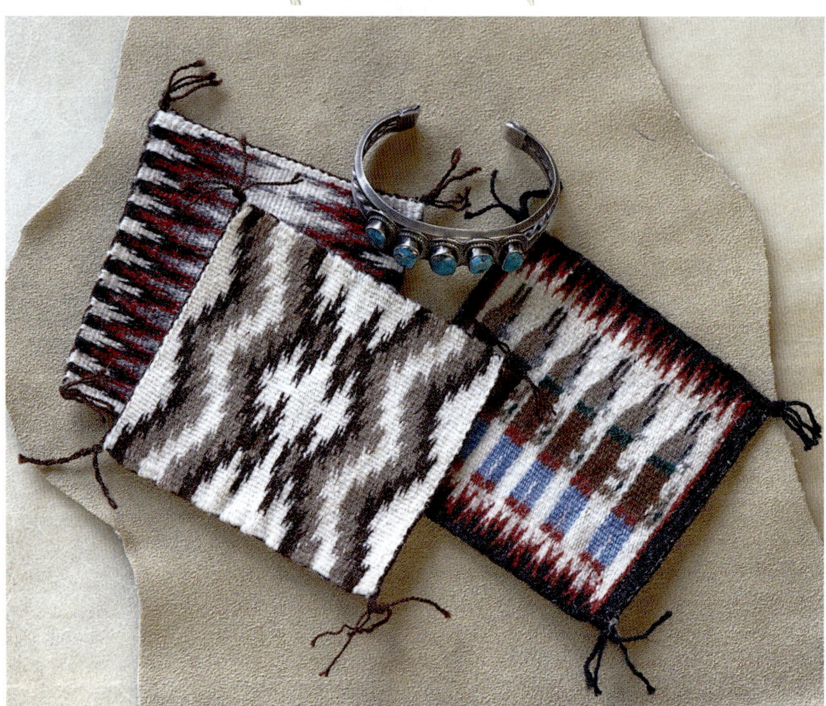

Figure 44. Two non-regional, geometric design miniature weavings by Lula Brown. Both 3⅞ x 3⅝ in. Yé'ii Bicheii miniature weaving by Louise Yazzie. 3⅞ x 3⅝ in.

traditional Navajo loom. This greatly increases the speed and ease of the weaving process. These may be detected by examining them for knotted warp pairs (the

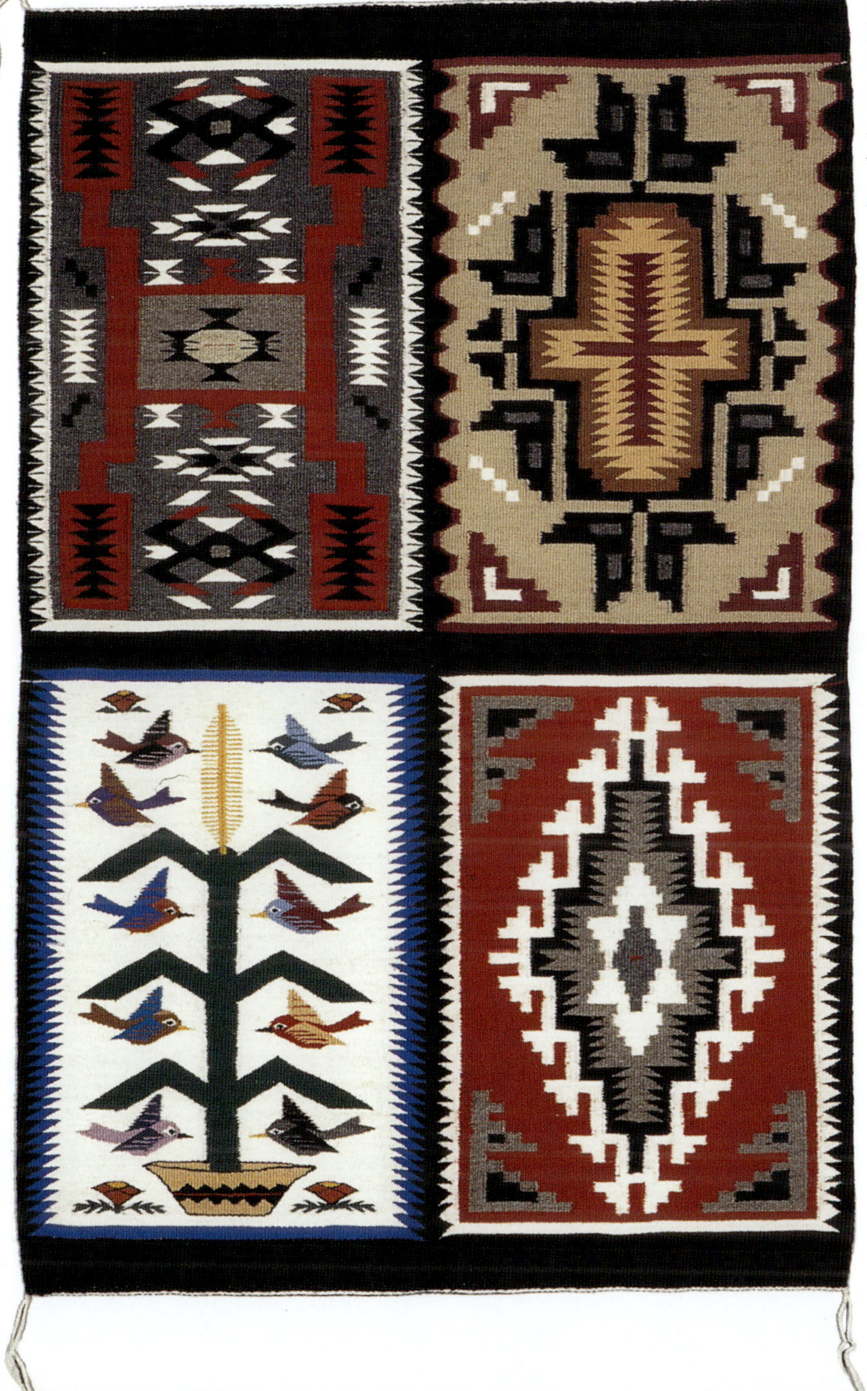

Figure 45. Four-in-one weaving by Priscilla Endischee. 42 x 28½ in. The textile includes (clockwise from the upper left): storm pattern, Teec Nos Pos variant, Ganado, and bird pictorial styles.

Figure 46. Rug-in-a-rug weaving by Priscilla Nelwood. 38½ x 27 in. A storm pattern rug seems to lie on top of a Wide Ruins weaving in this example.

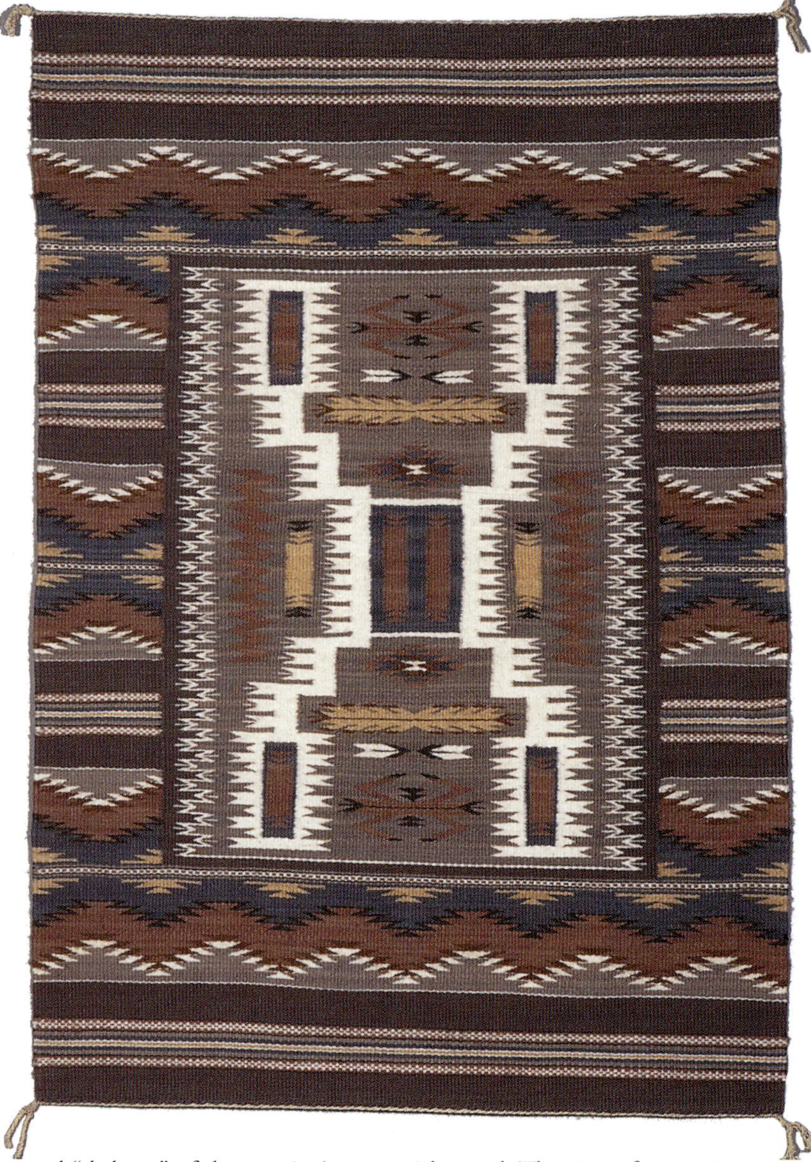

wool "skeleton" of the weaving) across either end. The sizes of true miniatures are often only 4 inches long by 3 inches wide. Some are even smaller. Patterns can be any of those used for a full-sized weaving. (FIG. 44)

MISCELLANEOUS PATTERNS

Sampler, or multiple-pattern rugs with designs of many different styles woven into the same rug, first appeared in the Transitional Period. For many years four-in-one rugs (four patterns on one weaving) were the most common form of sampler, although nine-in-one, fifteen-in-one, and other multiples are also seen. (FIG. 45) Another variation is the so-called rug-in-a-rug, where one pattern is symmetrically

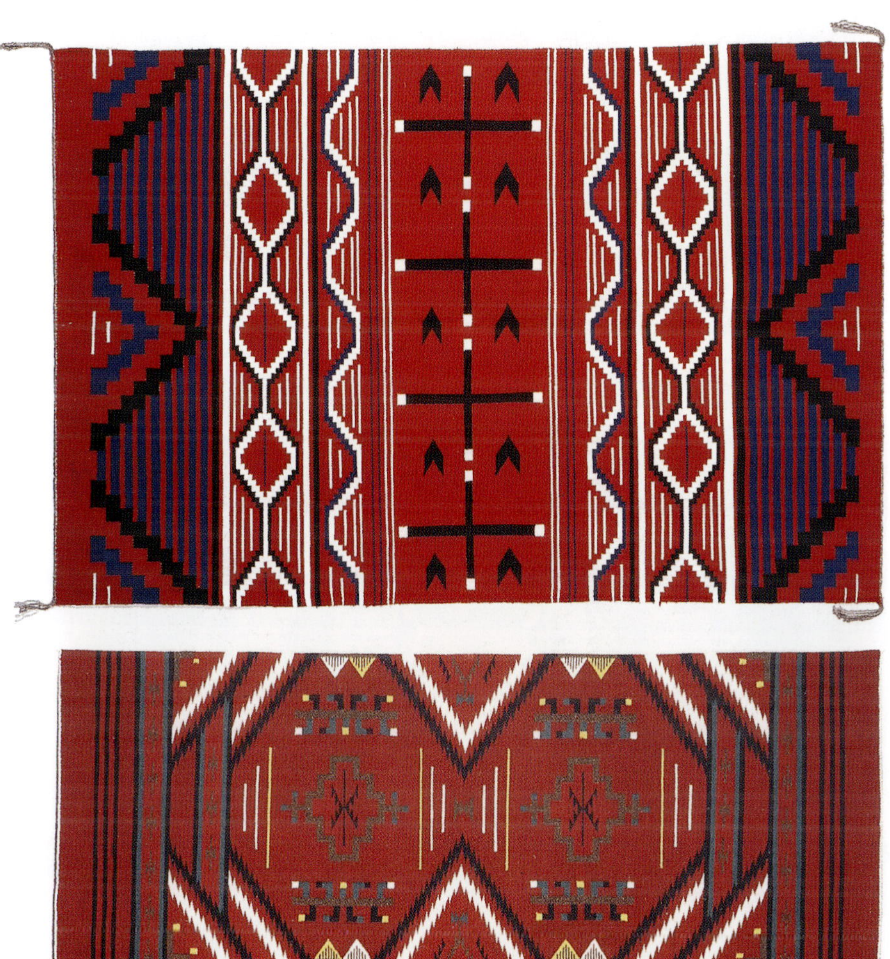

Figure 47. Classic wearing blanket revival weaving by Gladys Shepherd. 62½ x 41½ in. This piece is based on styles prevalent during the 1860s.

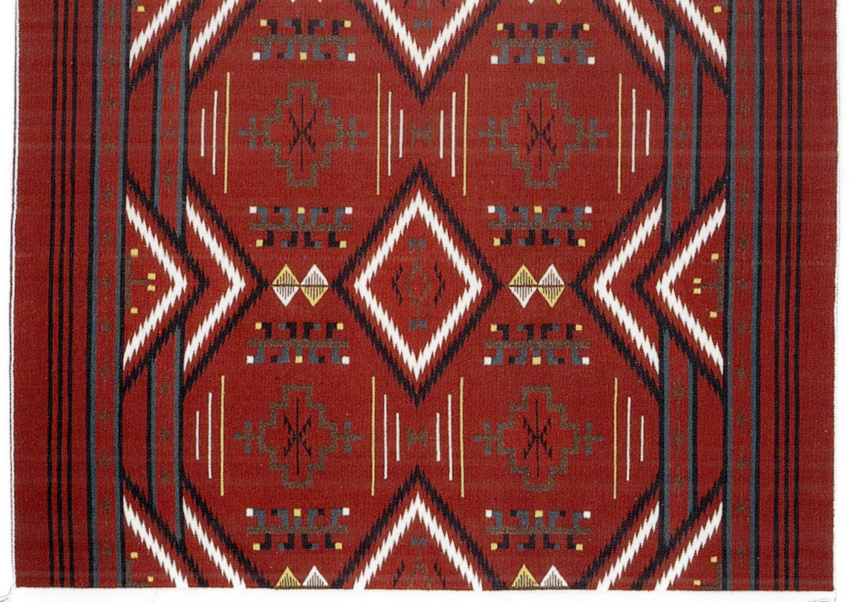

Figure 48. Germantown revival weaving by Sally Scott. 72 x 52 in. Chief's blanket influences with Germantown-type colors are both evident in this textile.

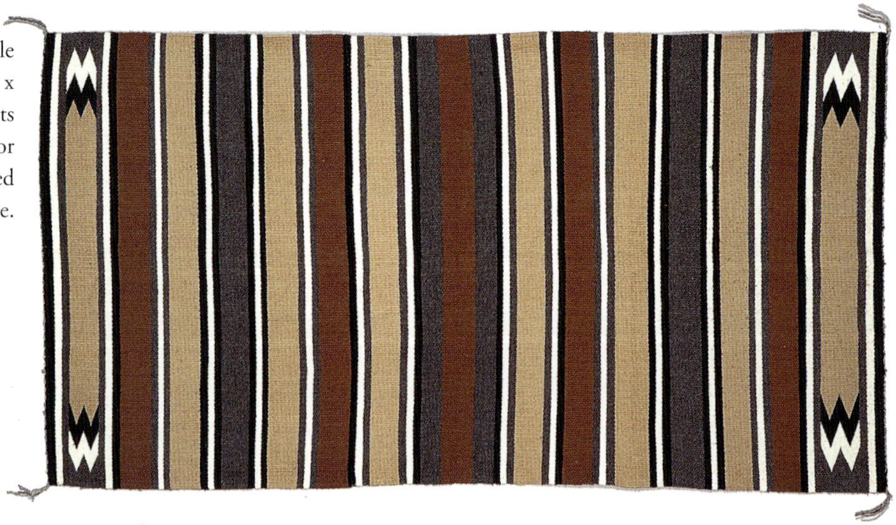

Figure 49. Double saddle blanket by Elvina Yellow. 58½ x 31 in. Typically, pattern elements are placed only in the corners or ends for visibility when used under a saddle.

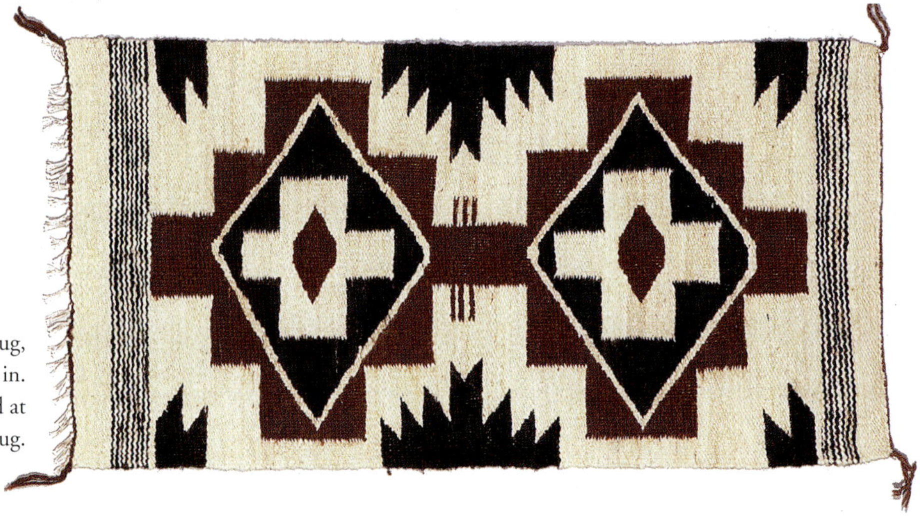

Figure 50. Gallup throw rug, weaver unknown. 36 x 18 in. Note the cotton warp exposed at one end of the rug.

centered over what appears to be another rug beneath it (often with a banded pattern). In some cases, the inner "rug" may even have tassels projecting from each corner on the front of the rug, heightening the illusion of a rug in a rug. (FIG. 46)

As in the past, Navajo weavers continue to produce revival patterns today. Especially popular are re-creations of Classic Period chief's and wearing blankets. (FIGS. 5 and 47) A newer trend developing in the 1990s has been a revival of weavings using the Germantown Transitional Period styles and colors. (FIG. 48)

UTILITARIAN WEAVINGS

We should also say a word about blankets for everyday use. In the Transitional Period, soft, loosely woven, striped blankets were produced for common uses, while the fancier wearing blankets were made to sell, to trade, or for special occasions. Saddle blankets in double (approximately 60 x 30 inches) or single size (30 x 30 inches) are often similar in weave and striping to the older utilitarian weavings. The Navajo certainly continue to weave saddle blankets for use on their own horses, but most are sold to non-Indians, often for use on the floor rather than a horse. (FIG. 49)

Gallup throws, woven and distributed primarily in the Gallup, New Mexico, area are also loosely woven. Their patterns are simple versions of different styles including stripes, geometrics, and Yé'ii figures. Because of their texture they are suitable for both floor and wall-hanging usage. Most of them have an exposed cotton warp fringe on one end. (FIGS. 50 and 51)

The tufted weave rug is a more unusual type. Alternate strands of goat hair are woven in with the weft threads to give a one-sided, shaggy rug. Tufted weave rugs are used both as saddle blankets and as sitting cushions while weaving. (FIG. 52)

We have tried to give a brief overview of the vast array of weavings that Navajo artists are producing today. Constant change permeates all styles of Navajo weaving, so categorization will continue to evolve. We hope we have given the buyer some basic knowledge to identify regional, pattern, and functional styles when looking at a roomful of rugs.

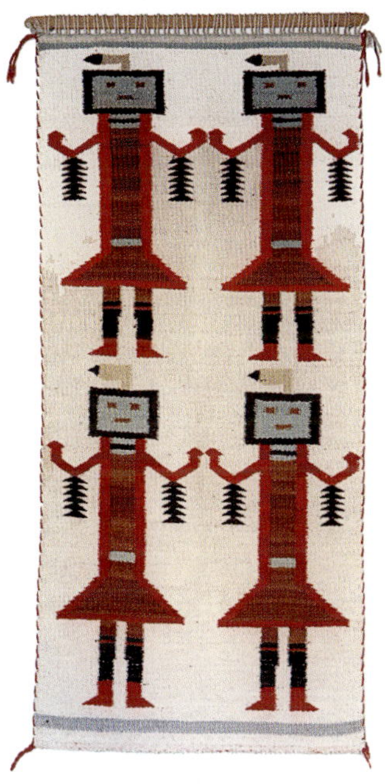

Figure 51. Gallup Throw rug, weaver unknown, circa 1950. 40 by 18 in. The weaving has four vertical Yé'ii as opposed to the more common horizontal row of Yé'ii.

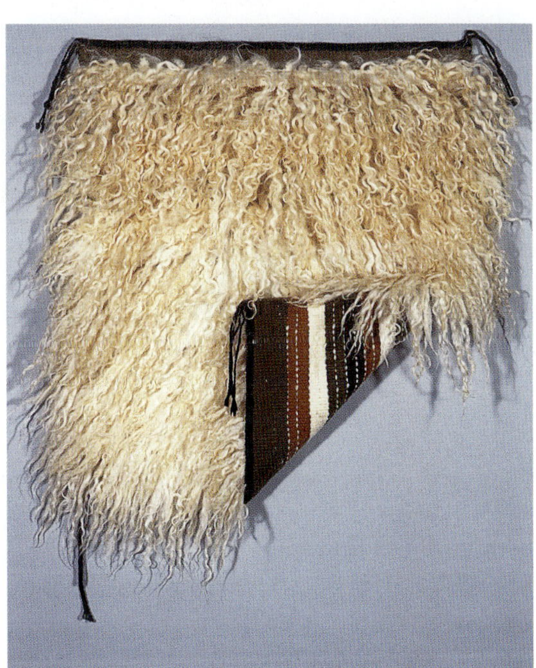

Figure 52. Tufted weave rug by Elsie Nez. 25½ x 22 in. This weaving is somewhat unusual in that it has a pattern on the back.

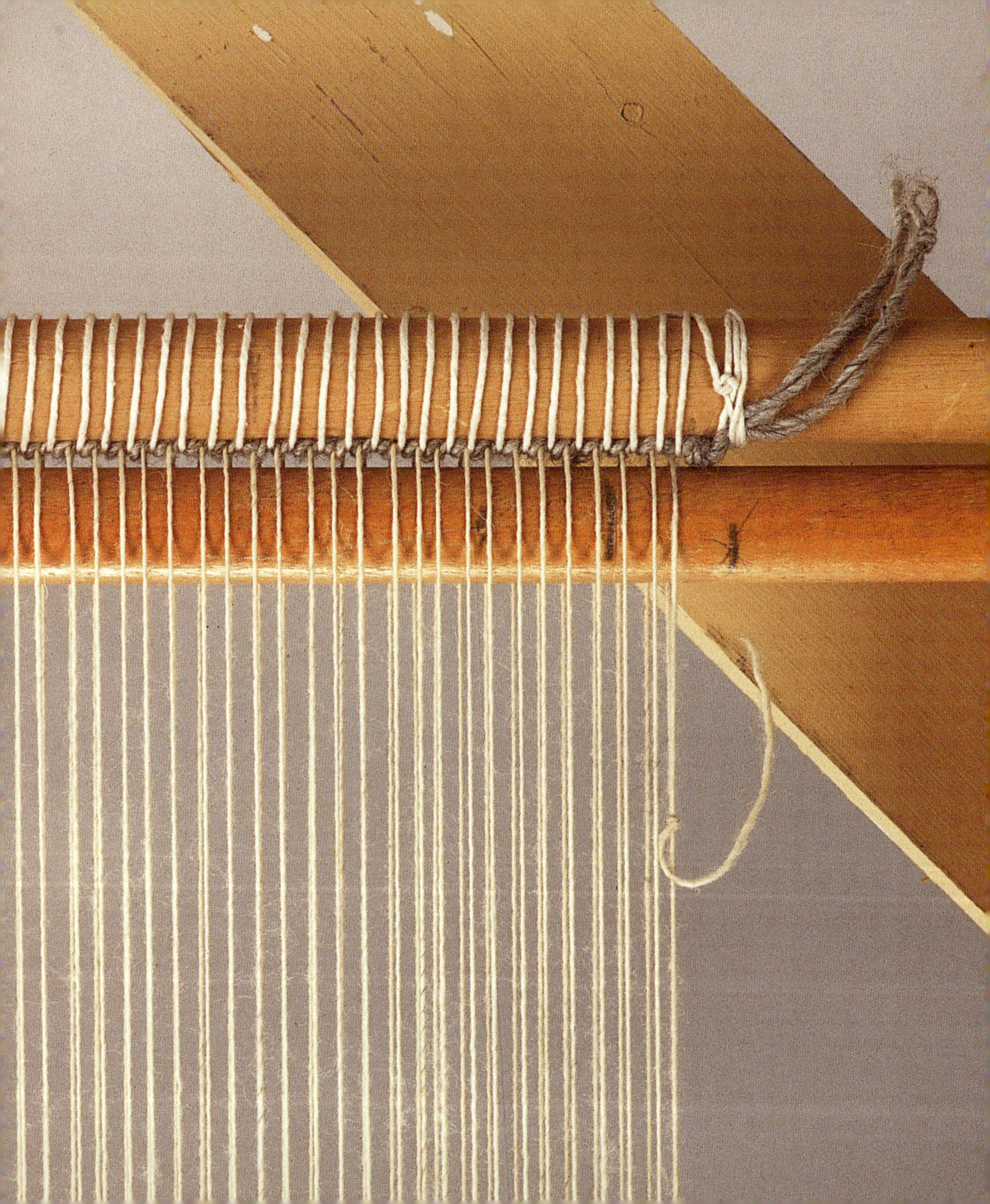

This is due primarily to their unique construction. Unlike the products of any other type of loom, Navajo weavings have four closed selvage edges. Other looms can produce only two (or, in rare cases, three). What this means is: no loose ends, no fringe, and no weak points at the edges of the weaving. The process involved in achieving the fourth selvage is unbelievably tedious, however, and requires years to master. Hence the difficulty of the process and the time involved in accomplishing the closed-edge phenomenon are major factors in the cost of a well-executed Navajo weaving.

Nowadays, Navajo weavers work on sturdy, usually rectangular loom frames. These are often constructed from finished lumber (two-by-fours or four-by-fours, for example), although some weavers prefer steel pipe or some other sufficiently strong material. Originally, looms were formed in one of two ways: either the weaver buried the ends of two logs vertically into the ground and then lashed strong cross beams horizontally to them (one near the tops of the logs and another near the bottoms, just above the ground); or, he or she may have found a thick, approximately horizontal tree branch, sufficiently high off the ground for the purpose. Strong ropes were tied around two or more fairly large rocks, which were then buried in the ground in a line parallel to the tree branch, with the ropes projecting from the ground. These ropes could then hold the bottom beam of the loom-to-be, while the top was secured to the tree itself.

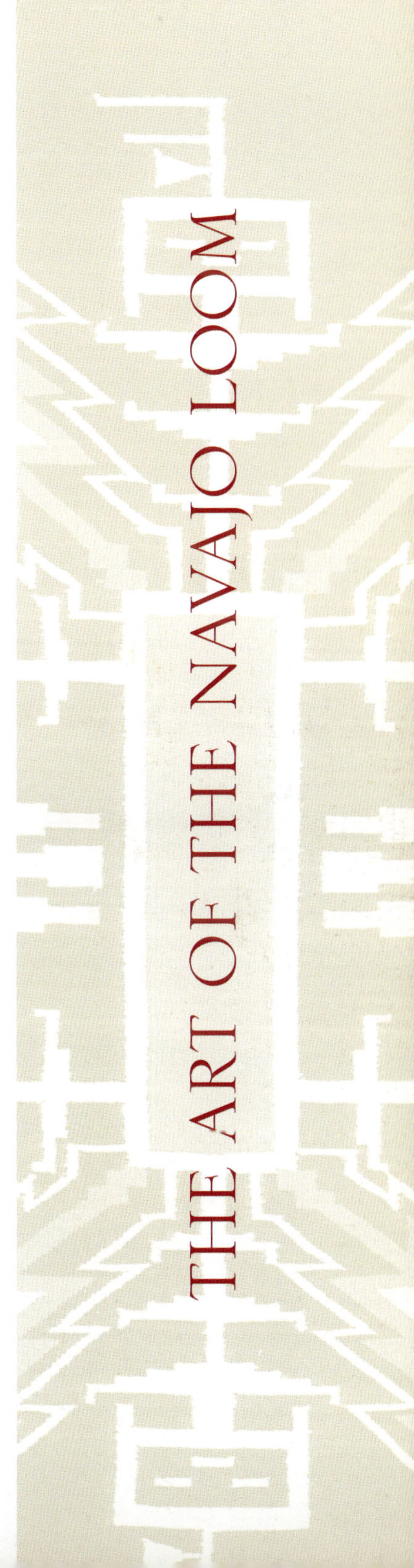

Regardless of the form of the outer frame, "warping" (the stringing of the "skeleton" of the weaving) is always done on a frame laid out horizontally. Sometimes (as with a contemporary loom) this frame is the loom itself. In older days, the weaver would construct a temporary warping frame, which was usually worked on the ground. (Today, most weavers will raise the frame onto four sufficiently tall objects to allow more comfortable work, as most no longer sit on the ground.)

Two temporary warp beams are attached to the frame, somewhat closer together than the desired length of the finished weaving. (Closer because the warp will stretch considerably as the loom is tightened prior to beginning the weaving process, and indeed, to a somewhat lesser degree, throughout at least the entire first half of the weaving.)

The weaver then ties one end of the warp in a loop around an end of one of the beams. The ball of warp yarn (which should be large enough to finish the entire structure, so as to avoid a knot in the warp within the weaving) is then passed alternately "out" over and then back "in" under the first one, then the other beams in a series of figure eights (FIG. 53). This stringing of the warp is the most critical

Figure 53. This side view shows the unique figure-eight structure of the warp of a Navajo weaving stretched on temporary beams.

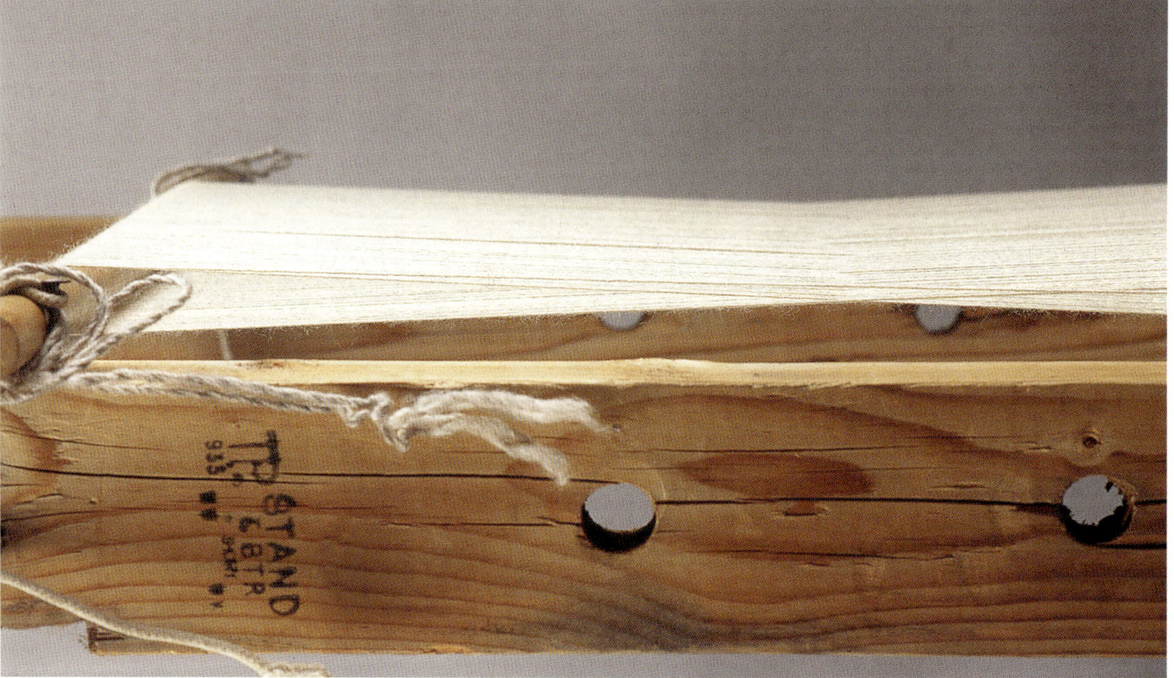

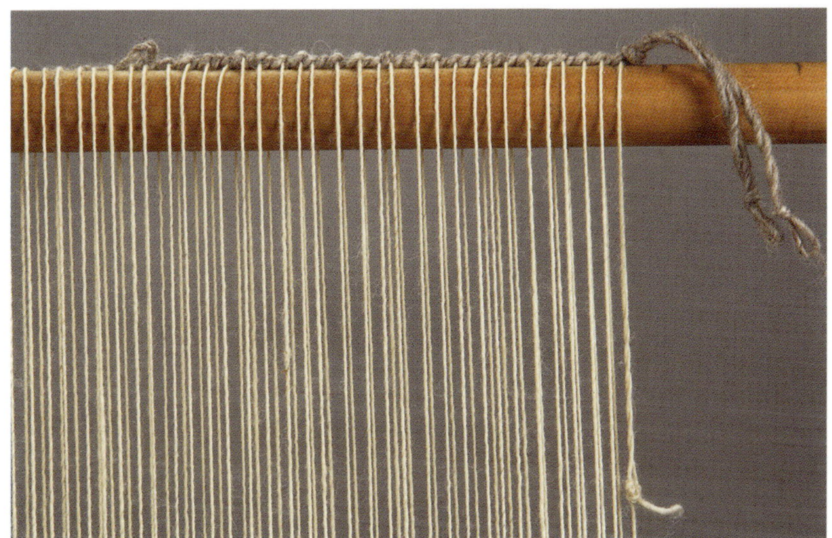

Figure 54. The edge-cord binding which will be the finished end of the rug.

step in the entire process. Each turn of the warp must be spaced as consistently as possible and (even more important and more difficult to achieve) each stretch of the warp from beam to beam must be as close to exactly the same degree of tension as every other. Mastering this process requires years of practice. The consistency of the warp might be compared to the proper stretching of a canvas for a painter. One cannot paint properly on an uneven canvas. Likewise, the best of weavers would have great difficulty working on an inconsistent warp. This is why, at least when a student is first learning the weaving process, warping is usually done by the teacher.

When the warp has been strung for the entire width of the weaving, the end is attached to one of the beams (the same as at the start if the weaver wants an even number of warps, the opposite if an uneven number is desired).

The end of the warp turns are then bound together with larger, extra-strength edge-cord yarns (FIG. 54). Each of these edge cords (two for each end of the weaving, which are essential to the foundation structure, and at least two more for each side if the weaver desires "side selvages") is usually made by twisting two or more strands of weft yarn tightly together, soaking them in hot water, and stretching them to dry, yielding very strong "two-ply" yarn.

The binding together of the warps is begun by passing one of the edge cords under the first turn of the warp at one edge of the weaving. The two edge cords are

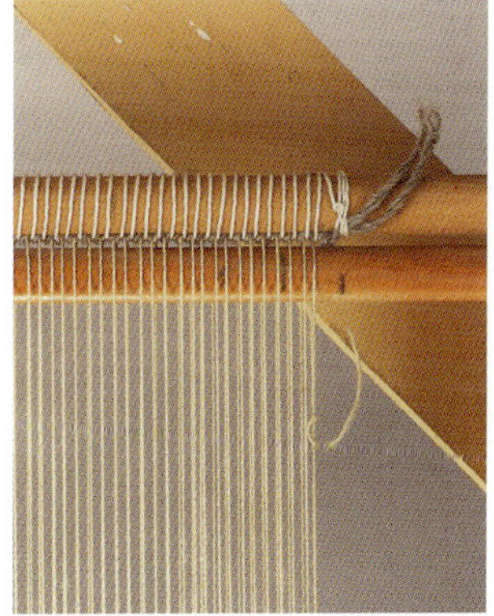

Figure 55. Lacing, end bindings, and warp structure on the permanent warp beam, with the temporary beam still in place. See page 54 for a larger view.

Figure 56. The Navajo loom.

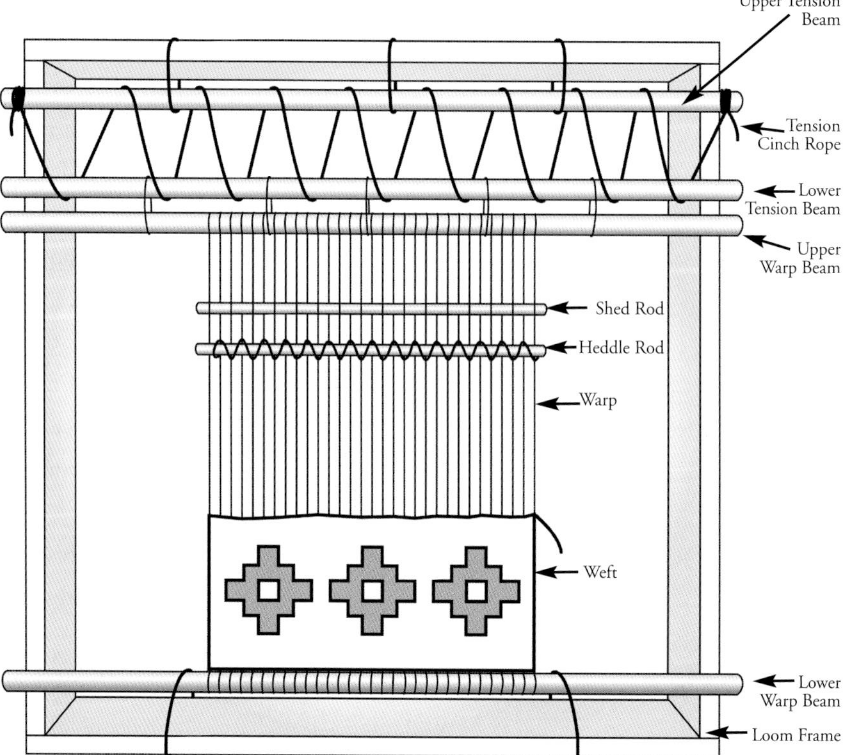

then twisted with each other, and the number of twists permanently sets the spacing of the warp turns. The cord then passes under the next warp turn, and so on across the width of the weaving. The process is then repeated at the other end of the piece.

Finally, the warp structure is transferred from the temporary beams to the permanent ones with a lacing cord (not part of the finished weaving), which passes around the beam, then around the selvage cords between each turn of the warp. (FIG. 55) Thin dowels (in older times, smoothed, usually willow, sticks) are then carefully inserted into the spaces in the warp structure (the "loops" of the figure eights) held open by the temporary warp beams. These will retain the "sheds," the two opposite spaces through which weft yarns will be alternately passed. The temporary beams are then removed, and the entire warp structure is mounted to the loom. The bottom beam is secured directly to the frame. The top beam is then connected by loops of wire (or strong cord) to an additional "tension" beam. A simple cinch-rope laces this beam to the top of the loom. (FIG. 56) This allows for tightening (or, in rare cases, loosening) the entire warp structure by pulling each turn of the cinch from one side to the other across the width of the loom and re-securing the end. Some weavers today have abandoned the rope in favor of modern hardware "turn-buckles." Most have not.

All of these factors (consistent spacing and tension of warps, consistent application of the end selvage cords, consistent and very tight lacing of the selvages to the beams) affect the quality of the final product. In addition, such elements as the thickness of the warp itself, and primarily, the diameter and degree of twist of the weft yarn are what determine the "fineness" of the weave. When we say a piece is "tightly woven," what we mean is that the warp is thin and closely spaced, and that the weft is very fine.

Warps per inch may vary from as few as four or five to as many as twenty or more. Wefts per vertical inch can range from as few as six or seven to as many as

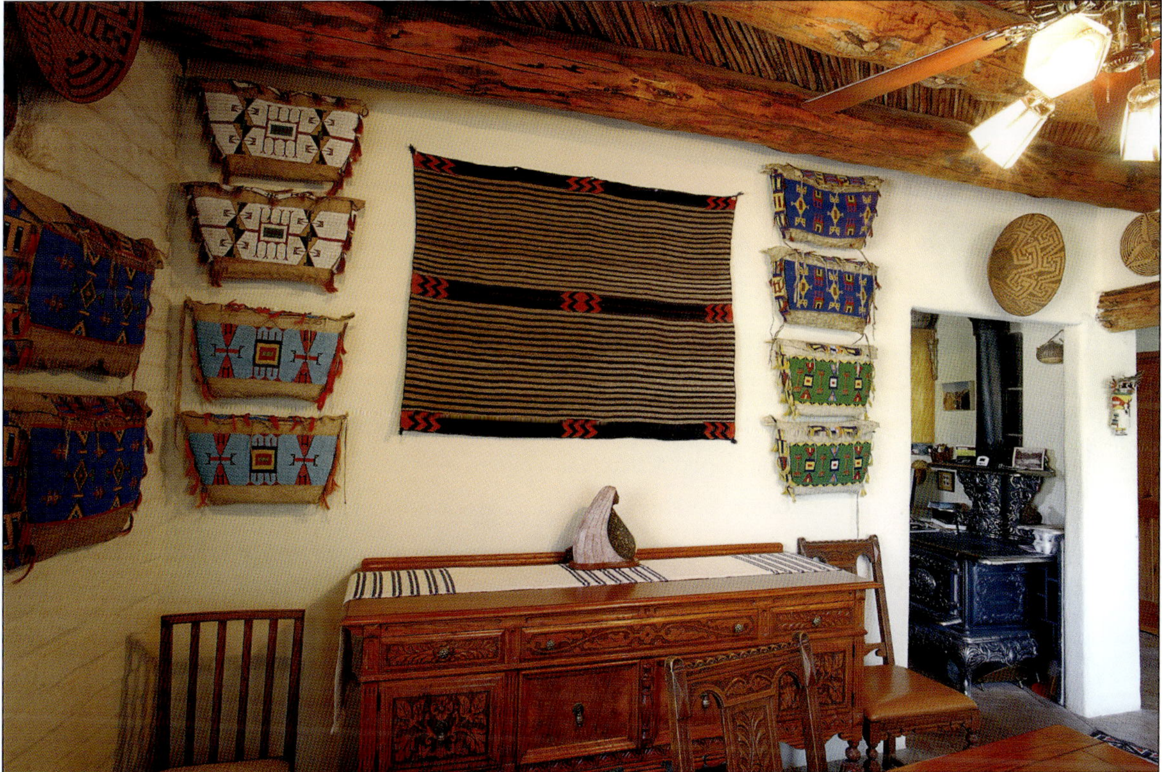

one hundred or more. Thin warp (properly spaced) and thin weft will create a "tapestry" fine wall hanging. Heavier warp and heavier weft (tightly spun) will make a floor rug. Widely spaced warps with looser, thicker weft will result in such pieces as "Gallup" throws, saddle blankets, or the famous (and now much sought after) Transitional Period blankets.

Before the weaving may begin, there is one more required step. The upper of the two dowels in the warp will be the holder of one of the two sheds (usually referred to as the "stick shed"). However, the lower one must be used to create the opposite space (known as the "pull shed") by attaching all of the warps it lifts to a "string heddle." This is accomplished with a series of string loops, which pass first around an additional dowel (the "heddle"), then around every other warp (those which are behind the top, or "shed rod" dowel) across the width of the warp structure. When this "heddle rod" is in place, the temporary lower shed dowel is removed. Then, and only then, is it time to begin the actual weaving process.

We should note here that the Navajo loom is quite different from the looms used by all other weaving cultures. The lack of any automated parts (foot peddles, machine-made heddles, beater bars, shuttles, tension cranks, etc.), so common on other looms, requires of the Navajo weaver a labor-intensive procedure, which is unimaginable to most other weavers. A Navajo rug is literally produced totally by hand. The "machine" that is the loom never stands between the weaver and the wool. (Fig. 57)

In most Navajo rugs, the basic technique employed is known as "tapestry" weave. This means "over one warp, under one warp," not a rug you hang on the wall. By this definition, all Navajo weavings (except twills and "two-faced" rugs, weavings which require four sheds), are tapestries. However, the term is also used by most rug dealers and collectors to designate super-fine weavings. (See the "Navajo Weaving in the Twentieth Century and Beyond" chapter.)

As the weaver works, he or she uses a batten (a smooth, flat, slightly-pointed stick) to hold the sheds open for the passage of the weft. Each strand of yarn is laid in individually and beaten into place with a wooden fork or comb. (FIG. 58) In a rug of even average complexity, there may be dozens of color changes (each requiring a different weft) on virtually every row. A typical contemporary piece (60 inches long, for example) may have anywhere from 1,800 to 3,000 or more rows of weft.

This individual placement of the yarns creates the pattern. Each weft is woven back and forth by hand, only within its own color area, interlocking with its neighboring color or turning on a common warp shared by that neighbor. On shuttle looms, used by most non-Navajo weavers, wefts are usually carried all the way across the width of the fabric, appearing on the back of the weaving wherever they do not show on the face. It is this process that creates the reversible effect in Navajo weaving that many find so remarkable. With few exceptions (twills, which display a reversal of colors on the "back," two-faced weaves, which are either partly or completely different when reversed, and raised outline weaving, which displays the raised design outlines only on the face of the piece) both sides are identical.

One of the most difficult aspects of Navajo weaving involves the fact that, as the weaving nears completion, the space within which the weaver must work grows ever smaller and tighter. Consequently, the weaver must use a series of smaller and

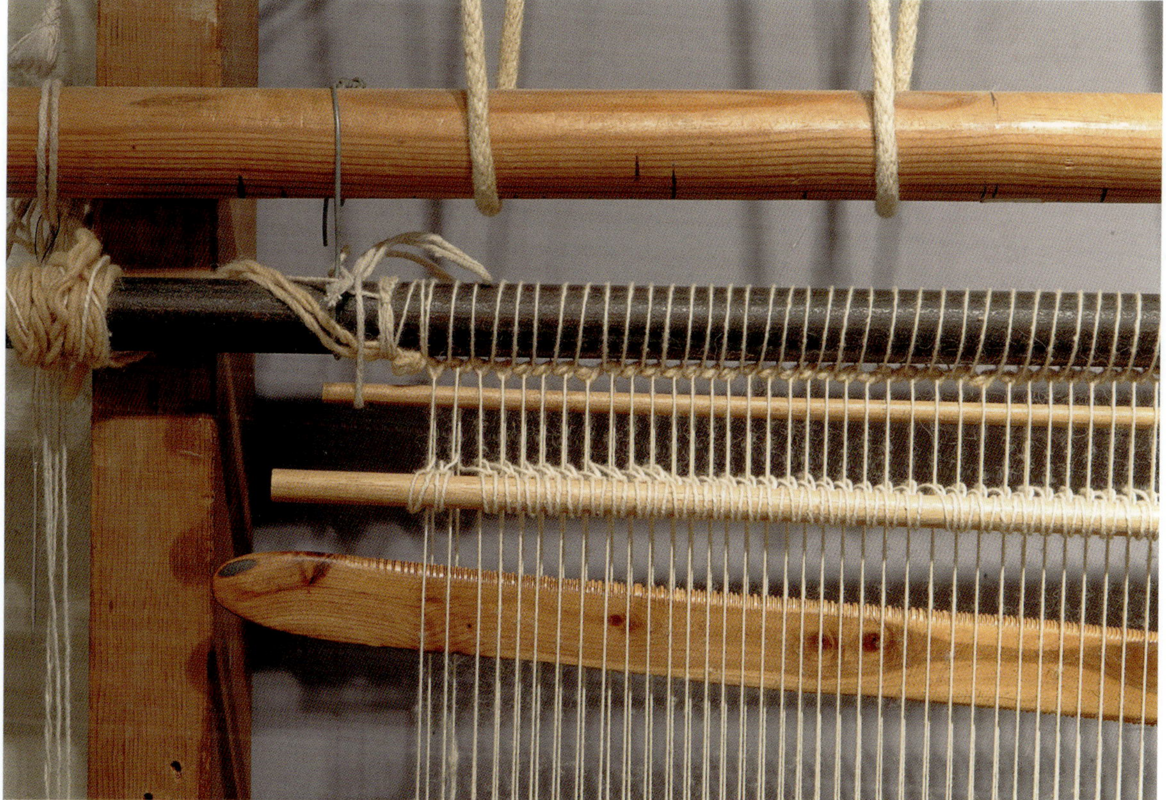

Figure 57. Top to bottom: Tension beam, upper warp beam, shed stick, string heddle, and batten.

Figure 58. The weaver's tools. Bottom left to top right: forks, needles, battens, Navajo hip spindle, and tow cards, shown on a Germantown revival weaving by Priscilla Warren. 36½ x 27 in.

smaller tools. Most weavers will progress through about five battens (the final one being a large needle) and at least three beaters. Eventually, the weaving is finished, literally one stitch at a time, using a curved needle (FIG. 59). Because of this labor-intensive process, the last few inches may require many days to complete. At this point, the difficulty and seemingly unending tedium may tempt the weaver to put in fewer rows, thus lessening the tightness of the finished product. However, the experienced weaver recognizes that a "good finish" is one of the qualities sought by knowledgeable buyers.

The most frequently asked question we hear is: "How long does it take to weave a rug?" There is no single answer. It takes as long as it takes. Fineness of yarn, intricacy of pattern, and the size of the rug will all affect the time required.

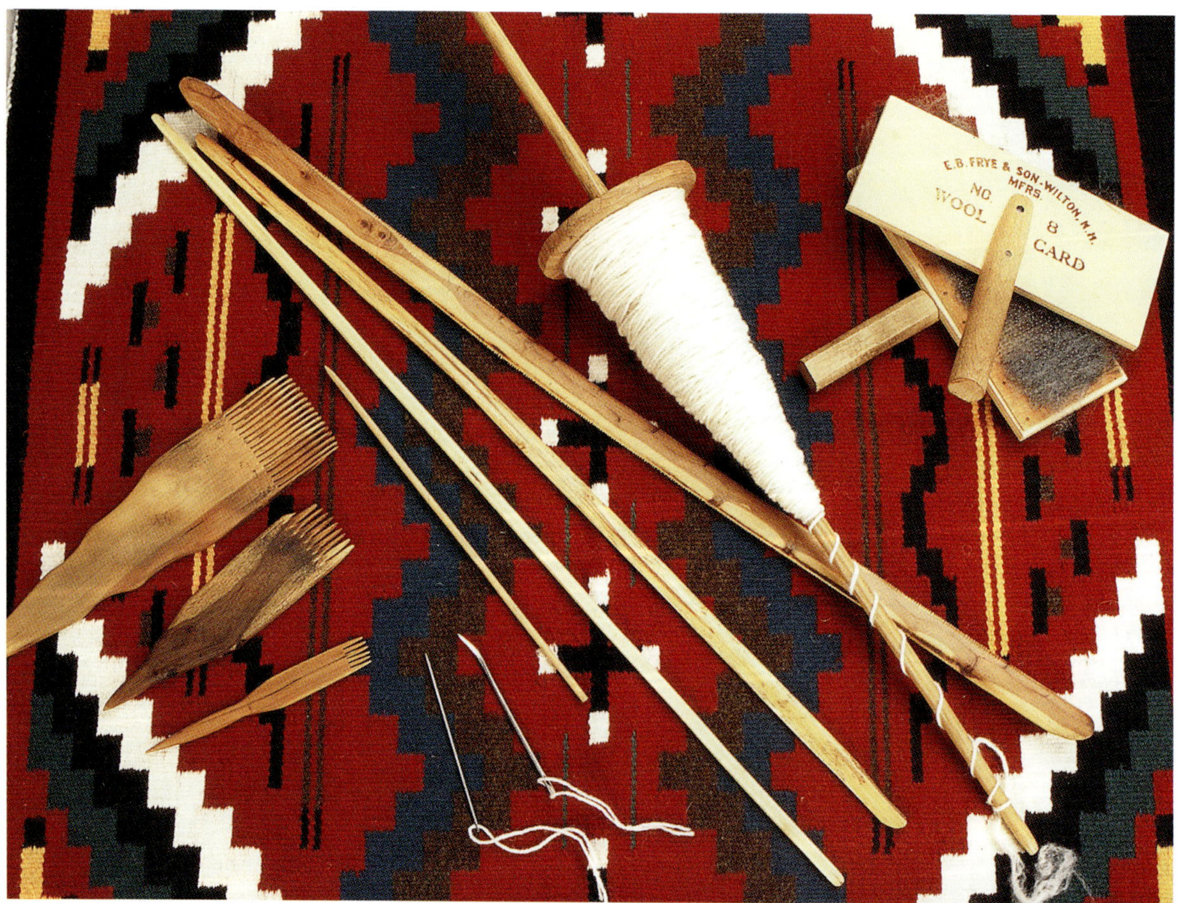

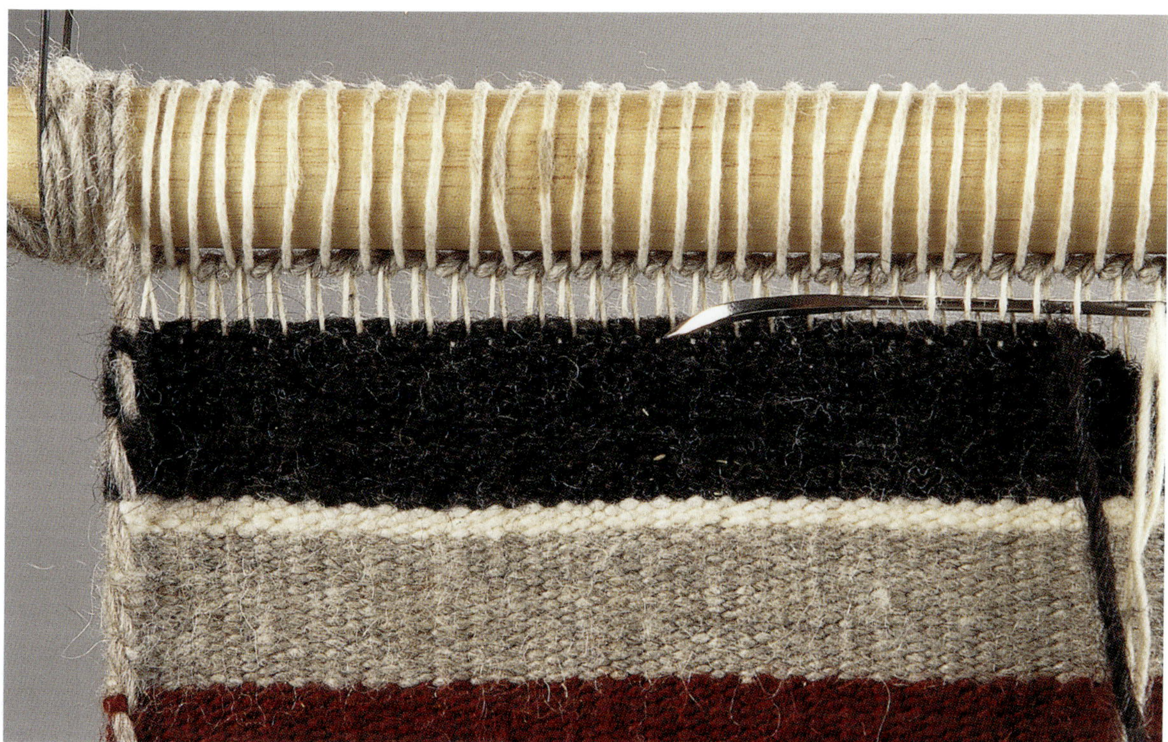

The health, strength, and age of the weaver also play a part; and some weavers simply work faster than others. The ultimate point, of course, must be the quality of the piece, not the speed of production. Suffice it to say that a Navajo weaver thinks not in terms of hours, but of the weeks, months, or perhaps years that the rug will be on the loom.

A point to consider regarding the time involved in a particular weaving is the source of the yarn. A weaver who prepares yarn "from scratch" has invested an enormous amount of time before the weaving of the rug has even begun. Shearing, washing, carding (raking the wool repeatedly between two heavy wire-toothed combs to align the fibers), spinning, and dying wool (not to mention gathering and preparing dyestuffs) is slow and demanding work. Homespun Navajo yarn is prepared on a simple hip spindle. (FIG. 58) The Navajos have never accepted the European spinning wheel, primarily because it is not as portable as the spindle. It is difficult to herd a flock of sheep while carrying a spinning wheel. Unfortunately, the time required for home production of yarn is rarely adequately reflected in the

Figure 59. Curved needle used to carry the final wefts between the warps.

price received for the rug. Consequently, most weavers today work with pre-spun yarn, conserving time for the more creative part of the process: the weaving. Some will use pre-dyed colors "as is," some dye their own using vegetal dyes, packaged dyes, and/or everything from Kool-Aid to powdered ladies' rouge.

STANDARDS OF QUALITY

Purchasing a Navajo rug can be a confusing and intimidating experience. Unless you are an expert, you must be able to rely on your dealer. Find one or two dealers in quality weavings who have done their homework and know how to tell good from bad. They should be able to demonstrate and explain the difference of styles, yarns, weavers, and the like. Check out their reputation, experience, quality of selection, etc. A knowledgeable dealer can tell you, for example, why two rugs of the same size, which may appear similar in design, have vastly different prices. If they cannot, go elsewhere! Ultimately, it is up to the prospective buyer to read, look, and ask questions. In this way, you can then be confident in your own knowledge and of the reliability of your dealer.

In judging the technical quality of any contemporary Navajo weaving, we advise that these standards be applied:

1. *Does the rug have straight edges and square corners?* It may be surprising how often this is not the case. While total straightness and squareness is the ideal, completely straight sides are somewhat of a rarity. To those accustomed to machine-made products, this may seem strange. In hand weaving, however, one of the most difficult aspects for the weaver to master is the control of a "clean" (straight and consistent) edge. Keep in mind also that the longer the rug, the harder it is to maintain a perfect edge and the more forgiving one must be. (However, parallelogram or trapezoid-shaped weavings should be strictly avoided.) Check by folding the piece to see that both ends are the same width.

2. *Are the pattern lines within the rug straight and consistent?* Keeping long lines (both horizontal and vertical) straight and even while weaving can be quite difficult. With horizontal lines, the slightest variation in the spacing of the warp and/or texture or diameter of the weft can cause a line to waver. Long vertical lines, even more than horizontals, are exceedingly tricky for the weaver to deal with. They have a tendency to become uneven in width and loose in texture (as in "fat and

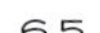

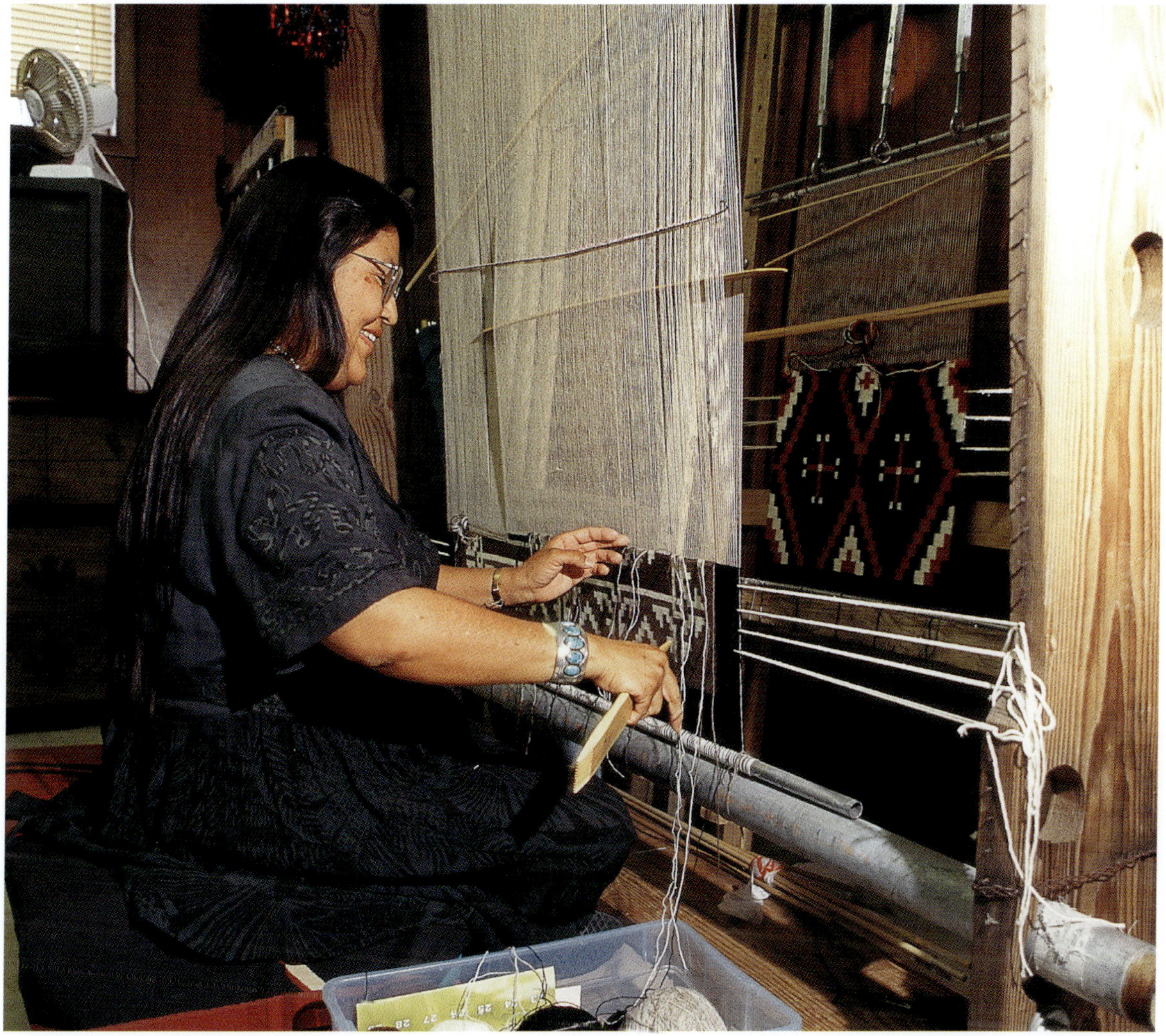

lumpy"). As an accomplished Navajo weaver once advised one of the authors, one must "pull tight at the line—and nowhere else!" Suffice it to say control of long lines indicates great skill on the part of the weaver.

3. *Is the pattern centered on the rug?* This may sound simplistic, yet placing the center of the pattern in the exact center of the weaving is much more difficult than might be imagined. Horizontal placement can be problematic (if warps are not spaced consistently) but is relatively simple compared to the "nightmare" of vertical centering. The weaving line in progress is always higher than it will be later on

Figure 60. Master weaver Barbara Teller Ornelas at her loom working on a Two Grey Hills tapestry, with a chief's blanket also in progress on another loom.

because the last several rows, although already beaten down with the fork, remain somewhat loose until compacted by more weaving above them. Since the warp is wool, it continues to stretch throughout the process, constantly extending the length of the piece. Humidity may also make the warps stretch. The weaver must consider all of these factors in determining the placement of the center of the pattern. Expertise comes only through years of experience.

4. *Will the weaving lie flat (or hang smoothly)?* As a general rule, avoid pieces with seriously curled corners, puckered edges, or ripples in the body of the weaving. Corner and side problems of this nature may or may not be correctable by an experienced restoration weaver. Ripples and puckers in the interior portion of the rug are usually impossible to remedy. At this point we must stress that a weaving should always be examined flat on the floor or hanging on the wall. Never purchase a piece that is shown only folded or draped or on a rack. In addition, always view the piece as you intend to use it (a floor rug on the floor, a wall rug hanging on the wall). Minor flaws that may not be noticeable on the floor may be glaringly apparent on the wall.

5. *Is the warp fully covered?* In the ideal Navajo weaving, the warp will be completely hidden. There are forgivable exceptions. Tiny bits of warp showing at the ends of the rug (where the body of the weaving meets the end binding cords) are acceptable. Exposed warp in solid color areas is the result of poor workmanship and should be avoided.

6. *Are there visibly noticeable "lazy lines"?* "Lazy lines" (inaccurately named by those who did not understand their function) are diagonal joints in the weaving, usually seen, especially in older rugs, in "background" color areas between design elements. They allow the weaver to work on a section of the rug for a period of time without having to move back and forth the full width of the rug on every row. A skilled weaver will insure that these joints are either totally invisible or at least barely noticeable in the finished product. Lazy lines have long been an accepted part of Navajo weaving technique. However, they should never be visibly distracting in a contemporary work. They sometimes now appear in revival weaving to give these pieces that old-time feel.

7. *Are the colors consistent?* In older weavings, color changes are a fairly common occurrence. In these pieces, yarn was usually home-dyed. Depending on the size of

the weaving (and the sizes of the largest dye pot available to the weaver), more than one dye lot was frequently required. Likewise, homespun wool inevitably came from more than one sheep. Sheep wool (just like human hair) varies considerably in degrees of oiliness, dryness, etc., resulting in the fact that different yarns hold dyes differently as far as long-term colorfastness is concerned. While two different dye lots may have appeared identical when new, over time they may have "mellowed" very differently. Hence, some of the marvelously character-lending color variations found in many older weavings. In contemporary weavings, color consistency is the norm unless the weaver has intentionally dyed for variegation in color.

In examining a weaving for all of the above-mentioned factors, the buyer must also consider the price. While the same standards are used to judge all weavings, they obviously must be applied more strictly to more expensive pieces. Flaws which may be somewhat forgivable in a $500 textile are not in a $5,000 one. Keep in mind also that the older the piece, the more lenient the application of the standards. The level of technical expertise demanded in Navajo weavings has constantly risen over the past hundred years or so. Likewise, the necessary use of such materials as tree branches in most older pieces resulted in, for example, less perfect ends than would today's dowels or pipes.

We should make a point here about budget. In the opinion of the authors, the buyer should usually seek out the highest affordable level of quality. It is better to have a very fine, smaller weaving than a larger but poorly woven one.

While all of the standards of quality are important, never overlook the emotional appeal of the piece. The artistic factor is paramount. If you love the weaving enough, it was meant to be yours. However, you must love it in spite of (and knowing) its possible technical imperfections. Flaws discovered after the rug is home can destroy your initial fondness for the weaving.

During the entire process of weaving, the weaver must be constantly alert to avoid any number of potential pitfalls. One must be aware at every turn of the weft at both edges to play the yarn, as one noted weaver said, "not too tight, not too loose," so as to maintain a straight side on the weaving. One must never pull interior design yarns too tight, as this too will cause a pulling in of the sides, resulting in an "hour-glass" shaped piece. The constant attention to vertical and horizontal lines has been mentioned previously. Attention to every placement of the batten is essential so as to prevent missing the pick-up of any warp and/or to avoid picking up a warp from the (currently) "back" shed. Either will result in "floating" or "skipped" stitches.

Try to avoid the pitfalls of "mystique." There are a number of persistent misconceptions (perpetuated, at least in part, by the sales pitches of some clerks and dealers) regarding Navajo weavings.

A classic example is symbolism. With the exception of Yé'ii, Yé'ii Bicheii, and sandpainting rugs, there is very little symbolic meaning behind the designs found in Navajo weavings. For the most part, they are simply beautiful patterns. While individual design elements may have acquired names over the years, these usually came about after the fact, due to a general resemblance to some object familiar to the viewer. Such a resemblance is usually coincidental, rather than intentional on the part of the weaver. On occasion, a weaver may create a geometric design that later reminds him or her of some particular item. For example, we once purchased a rug from an older Navajo weaver. She referred to an interesting design element that was used throughout the piece as "rabbit tracks." These were neither symbolic nor intentional. She had simply noticed, after the fact, the resemblance.

One very notable exception to the rule of no symbolism is the so-called "swastika" found in some rugs woven prior to World War II. To the Navajo, it is the "whirling logs" symbol that appears in a variety of ritual sandpaintings. It tells the story of a protagonist often called Self Teacher, who takes a hazardous river journey culminating in ceremonial knowledge for the tribe.

Another myth is the intentional flaw. This simply does not exist in Navajo weaving. It may be true that some Oriental rug-weaving cultures believe that "only God can make something perfect," and therefore their weavers introduce an intentional flaw into the pattern of each rug. This is certainly not true among Navajo weavers. Almost any Navajo weaving, if examined closely enough, will reveal at least one flaw, but this is not due to any religious taboo or cultural belief. It is because weavers are human and humans make mistakes.

The buyer must not confuse flaws, intentional or otherwise, with the phenomenon known as the spirit line (also called the spirit trail or weaver's pathway). This is a narrow line of weft yarn which allows the "escape" of the primary background color directly through all pattern and border colors to the edge of the rug.

The line is usually woven in at the point of the background color nearest to the right-hand edge of the rug as the weaver approaches the end of the weaving (Fig. 61). Most weavers will tell you that this opening allows their creativity, or the "good spirits" to flow out of the weaving, not to be "trapped," and to be available to them to use it again during the creation of the next weaving. You will sometimes hear or read that the spirit line allows the escape of "the evil spirits." This is simply not true. If a Navajo weaver believed that there was anything inherently evil involved in a weaving, he or she would not have anything to do with the entire process.

Weavers will tell you that the exit is "to the east." One theory states that in the days when much weaving was done outside (there is very little light in a traditional Navajo home, or "hogan"), a weaver would naturally orient the loom so that it faced south. The sun would be at the artist's back, not in their eyes. This would mean that "to the right" was "to the east." Openings, as perceived in Navajo culture (in sandpaintings and hogans, for example), are always to the east, for various cultural and religious reasons.

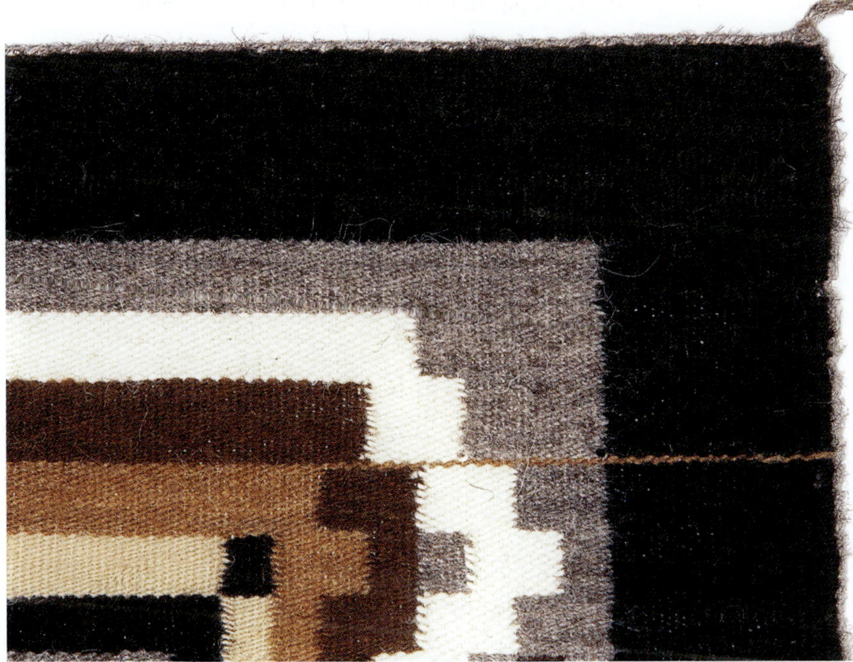

Figure 61. Close-up of a spirit line in a Two Grey Hills weaving by Dorothy Lowe. Note the extension of the spirit line from the brown background through the pattern and border colors to the rug's edge.

Caring for Your Weavings

Once you have found and adopted the rug that was meant to be yours, you must assume the responsibilities of being its keeper. Do not panic. The "care and feeding" of a Navajo rug is not difficult. There are, however, a few dos and don'ts which you must remember.

Don't ever wash a Navajo weaving! No matter what you may have heard or read about pioneers scrubbing their rugs in the snow, do not ever consider getting water on your rug. (Yes, they did scrub them, and yes, they did ruin them.) Wool is an organic material and all of the various types of cords that make up a Navajo rug (warps, wefts, selvages) will react differently to liquids. Some stretch, some contract. Water may cause puckers and ripples, or worse. Such damage to the basic foundation of the rug is often irreparable.

Don't snap or beat a Navajo rug. This can damage the natural fibers, also. At most, shake the rug gently, holding it only by the sides and never the ends.

Do vacuum the rug. Again, as wool is organic, it must be kept free of insect larvae and other potentially damaging dirt and debris. If the rug is on the wall, it should be taken down and gently vacuumed on both sides at least every six

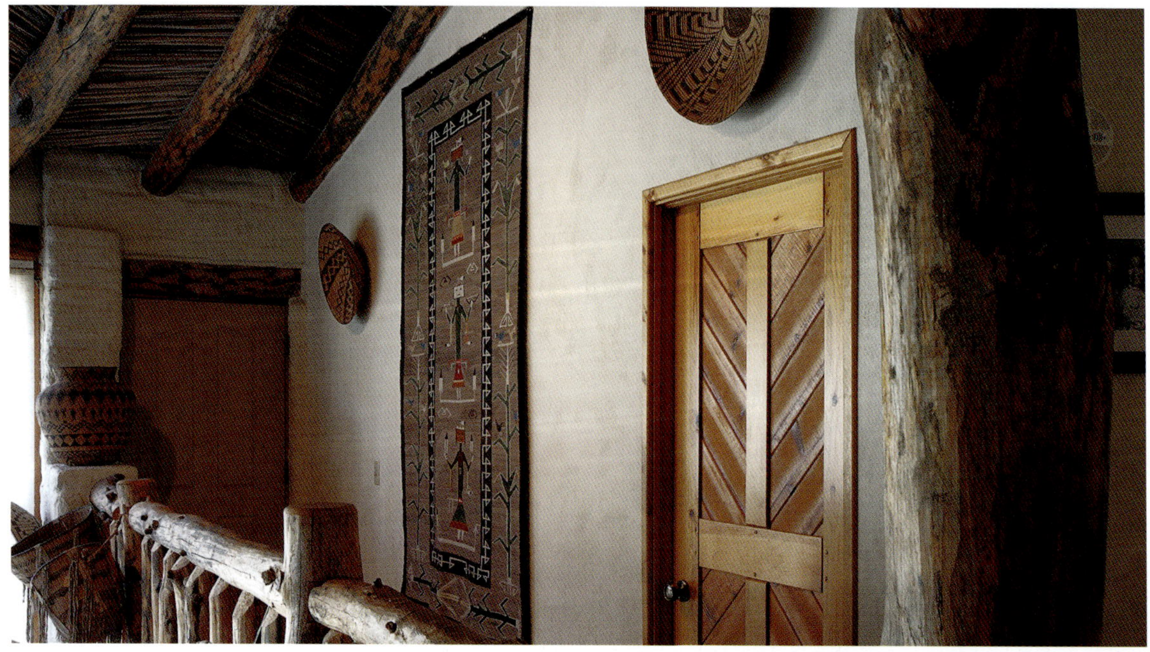

months. If on the floor, it will usually require more frequent cleaning. Use upholstery attachments, never a beater brush. Avoid corner tassels. Eventually, all floor rugs and some wall hangings may need professional cleaning. Check with your dealer for a reliable cleaner near you. If this is not possible, seek out the closest reputable cleaner of fine Oriental carpets and rugs (preferably one who has experience with Navajo textiles).

Do consider texture and traffic. Whenever a rug is used on the floor, the conditions and traffic of that area must be compatible with the tightness and thickness of the weaving. A rug that may be suitable in a guest bedroom, for example, may not wear well in an entryway.

Do rotate rugs periodically. Floor rugs should be turned in a different direction every time you vacuum. Wall hangings should be rotated (top to bottom, front to back) at six-month intervals when you take the rug down for vacuuming. We also recommend that rugs be given a *very light* "misting" with a moth-proofing spray at this time. (Remember that moths, silverfish, and especially crickets are your enemies.) With the weaving laid out at floor level, hold the spray container at approximately shoulder height and mist briefly (on both sides alternately) to avoid getting too much chemical residue on the piece.

Do use pads under floor rugs. Even on smooth floors, a minimum-thickness foam or felt (not plastic mesh), non-skid mat should be used to prevent sliding. On floors with any irregularities (tile, etc.), put down thicker pads.

Don't position floor rugs under heavy, abrasive, or sharp-edged pieces of furniture. If such placement is absolutely necessary, use furniture-leg cups and rotate the rug much more frequently.

Do use Velcro if the weaving is to be used as a wall hanging. In years passed, rug collectors were forced to do terrible things to their rugs in order to hang them. Now, thanks to the inventor of Velcro (who, it is said, was inspired by a thistle caught on his trousers), hanging a rug is neither difficult nor damaging to the fabric. Rug Velcro is different from clothing Velcro. Unlike the two-sided fasteners used on clothing and shoes, where one side has "hooks" and one has "loops," rug Velcro requires only the hooks. (The wool of the rug acts as the loops.) Rug Velcro is usually about two inches wide for a better hold on larger rugs. It has an adhesive backing which adheres directly to the wall. The Velcro may also be stapled, nailed, or tacked to the wall (with its backing) to avoid lifting paint with the adhesive. (Note: Sometimes old rugs are polished so smooth from use that they will not grip the Velcro. In such cases, ask your dealer for possible alternatives.)

Don't hang a weaving with nails, brads, staples, or "tack-strip" piercing the rug. Any such intrusion in the fabric of the rug may cause extreme damage. Metal points may puncture or tear the yarn, or may rust, causing permanent discoloration. No matter how closely spaced, such points of suspension will eventually cause sagging in between. This stretching, much like the damage from washing, is irreparable. An alternative means of hanging rugs involves two wooden presser bars (much like old-fashioned men's pants hangers). The problem with these is that they too may eventually leave permanent impressions on the rug.

Don't frame Navajo rugs under glass, plexiglass, or any other material that will prevent the natural "breathing" of the wool. Weavings that are sealed in may develop problems from mold, mildew, insects, etc. Additionally, don't ever allow a framer to glue a Navajo weaving to any sort of backing or matting. This prevents all maintenance and will destroy any value which the piece may once have had. There are acceptable methods of framing rugs, which will vary depending on the particulars of the piece. Check with your dealer regarding those techniques best suited to your needs.

Don't store rugs for any length of time unless it is absolutely necessary. If so, never store them folded, but always rolled. Rugs should be rolled from end to end, never from side to side. If possible, they should be rolled around something, such as a cardboard tube, to prevent excessive curling on the inside end. The rolled weaving should then be wrapped in acid-free tissue paper, white or brown wrapping paper, or a clean, plain white bed sheet. Never store a rug wrapped in plastic, as plastic can allow moisture to condense on the inside.

Do protect stored rugs against moths and other insects. Cedar-lined chests or closets are ideal. Otherwise, use moth spray (see above), flakes or balls, remembering to replenish these at six-month intervals. (Keep in mind that moth flakes and balls should never actually touch the rug.)

If problems occur with your rug, do not despair. Most can be remedied. Removal of stains and soiling is usually possible through proper cleaning. Discoloration due to the running of certain dyes in some old rugs (almost never a problem in contemporary weavings) can often be removed by a process called de-bleeding. Structural damage (some curling and rippling, holes, puppy-chewed corners, worn edges, etc.) can be remedied by a knowledgeable restoration weaver. Never allow anyone to repair your Navajo rug using sewing techniques such as darning. Such work can be undertaken only by those who have the necessary skills to fully restore Navajo weavings. Check with your dealer for assistance in locating a reputable restoration weaver.

Don't let these few requirements discourage you. The time and effort involved in properly caring for a fine rug are minimal. The pleasure such a piece will bring is vast. Above all, remember: Navajo weaving is an art form and should be viewed, used, and appreciated as such.

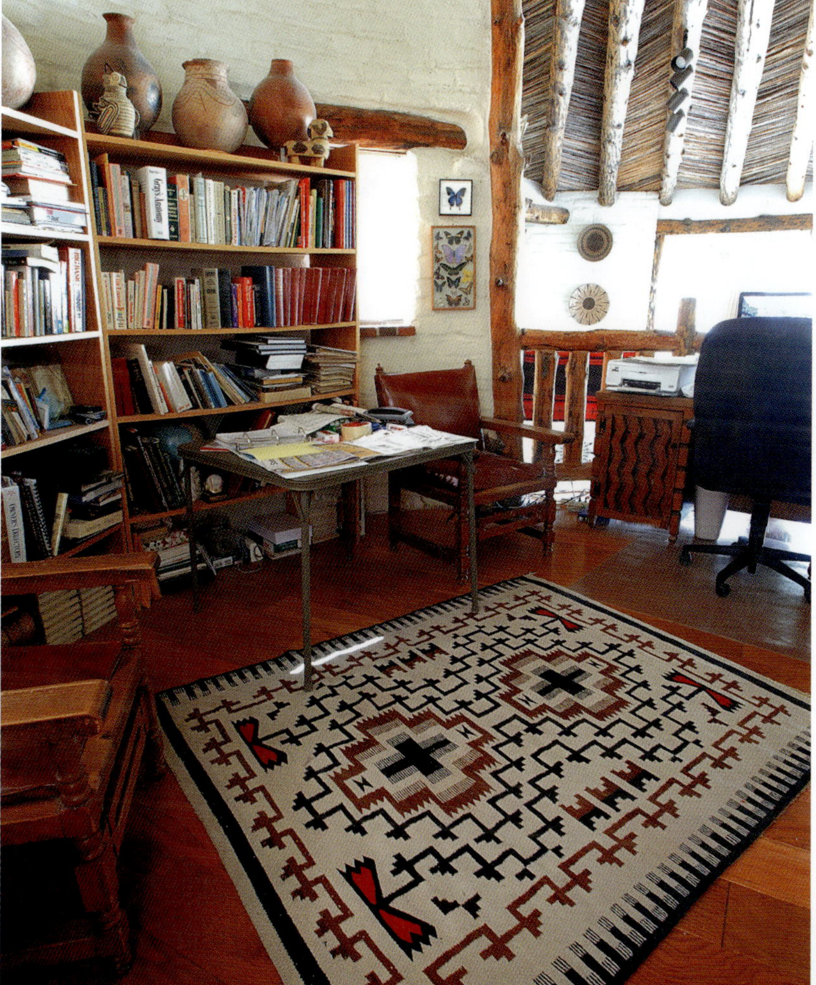

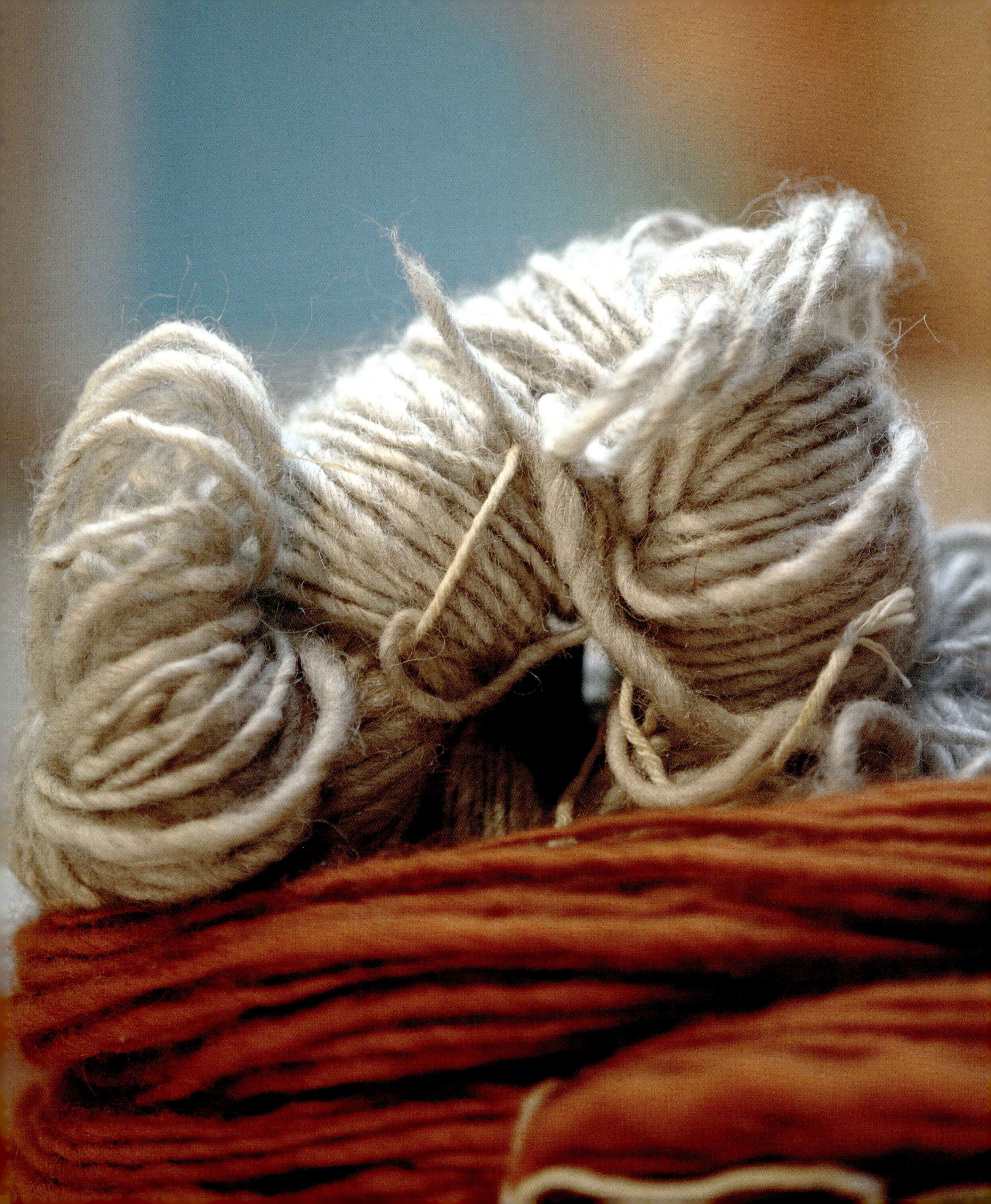

Over the years, the process of
weaving a Navajo textile and the loom
on which it is created have
changed very little.

The look and function, however, have undergone dramatic transformations. These changes have paved the way for an exciting future for the art of Navajo weaving.

As we have pointed out, Navajo women originally began weaving to make clothing and blankets to wear. Over time, these items were used as trade goods and, still later, as products to sell. Today, economic considerations have become the prime motivating factor in the continuation of Navajo weaving. This is not to deny that some artists, like Pearl Ben of Sweetwater, Arizona, weave in part because it is a hobby. Like others, she also weaves to continue the age-old tradition of weaving as part of the Navajo woman's role. Artists such as Barbara Teller Ornelas, originally from Two Grey Hills, New Mexico, have an almost physical need to weave. She says, "Weaving is in my soul….I do not feel right unless a rug is on the loom." Artistic expression is often another goal. For some weavers, the creative process itself is a reward totally apart from the financial one. Still, most Navajo weavers would not continue if they could not earn money in the process.

Creating a rug is a long and arduous task; hence, any time- or labor-saving innovations are of the utmost importance. The single most important change in this area has been the widespread distribution of commercially spun and dyed wool yarn. Two companies most responsible for this development were Brown's

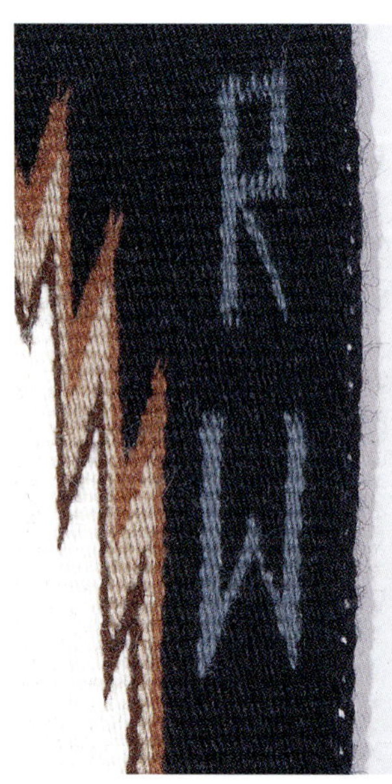

Figure 62. Close-up of a letter signature in a Yé'ii weaving by Ruby White.

Sheep Company of Mitchell, Nebraska, and John B. Wilde & Brother of Philadelphia, Pennsylvania. As of this writing, Brown's Sheep Company provides the majority of yarn used in Navajo textiles. Brown's started selling yarn in the Shiprock area around 1980. At first they offered only four colors, but the palette rapidly expanded and now includes many vegetal-looking shades. Today, according to Harlan Brown, about one-third of their yarn goes to Navajo weavers, distributed through several traders on the reservation.

The entrance of the Wilde company into the Navajo market came from a collaboration with trader Bruce Burnham of Sanders, Arizona. In the early 1980s, Burnham worked with Wilde's (in business since 1880) to produce what he calls "carpet yarn" that the weavers could use. They, too, started with about four colors but now make many hues. Burnham markets the yarn under the name "Wilde & Wooly." Burnham has recently purchased all of Wilde's wool and is now having it processed in New Hampshire. Some of it is home-dyed by Navajo women using vegetal dyes, as well as mixtures from other sources in a multitude of shades. We have heard of weavers using Kool Aid, grape juice, crepe paper, and lady's rouge, among others, in their dyes. Wilde & Wooly yarn is available in four weights from fine tapestry to saddle-blanket thickness.

Burnham and Wilde also marketed three-ply Germantown yarns in bright, old-style colors that duplicate the look of Transitional Period yarns, specifically for weavers wishing to create Germantown revival rugs. Unfortunately, unscrupulous individuals may try to age contemporary weavings using this yarn, in the hope of extracting a high price for a fake "antique." Wilde sold Burnham all of their remaining Germantown yarn, but Burnham says he is currently unsure whether or not there will be more unless he can find a mill to process the wool for him. The wool is from Lincoln sheep, which is a desert-adapted breed.

People often seem surprised to learn the extent to which most Navajo weavers use commercially prepared yarn in their rugs. Most traders estimate that about 95 percent of all contemporary Navajo weavings contain commercial yarns. It is difficult for many people to distinguish it from handspun yarn, but a knowledgeable and reputable salesperson should be able to show the buyer the difference. A buyer should assume that a contemporary rug does not contain handspun yarn unless it is specifically proven otherwise. Many dealers do not divulge this fact to their customers because of the romance of handspun and dyed yarns and fear of negative reactions to commercial ones. People forget that the Germantown yarns used well over a hundred years ago were also completely commercially manufactured, yet the rugs containing them are now very valuable.

Most important is the fact that there would be few Navajo rugs around today if weavers were not using commercial yans. Making a living from weaving would be virtually impossible without them. The process of carding, spinning, and dying wool takes a tremendous amount of time and significantly reduces the ratio of money received to effort spent. The elimination of wool preparation before weaving has also allowed artists the flexibility to focus on more intricate designs and to create some of the most consistently textured and evenly finished rugs ever made.

Navajo-grown wool is still being processed, although fewer and fewer trading posts are purchasing it, according to trader Kent Morrow of Shiprock Trading Post in Farmington, New Mexico. Currently Navajo churro wool is bringing the highest price. Churro sheep have gradually been reintroduced to the Navajos thanks to several Navajo and non-Navajo individuals and groups. Churro wool, less greasy and longer-fibered than the more commonly used Navajo merino sheep wool, is gaining favor among some weavers. Certain dealers have also championed its use. Stephen Pickle of Hubbell Trading Post in Ganado, Arizona, says that they are even raising churro sheep on the grounds. However, due to the limited number of Navajo churro sheep, widespread usage and general acceptance among the mainstream of Navajo weavers remains to be seen. Trader Jackson Clark II of Toh-Atin Gallery in Durango, Colorado, says most weavers simply don't want to handspin their yarn anymore because they don't really get any extra money for the process.

Unlike potters or Hopi katsina doll carvers, Navajo weavers rarely sign their pieces. Most buyers cannot tell one artist's textiles from another's. Thus, in recent years some traders have attempted to induce artists to weave in signatures (whether letters or symbols), usually in one corner of the piece. So far this signing is limited to a very small number of weavers. Most Navajo have resisted, since anonymity (which safeguards the power associated with one's name) and non-competitiveness are both deep-seated traditions. Some traders regularly insist on signatures when they purchase a rug. It may one day become common practice, given the Anglo preference for signed artwork of all kinds. (FIGS. 62 and 63)

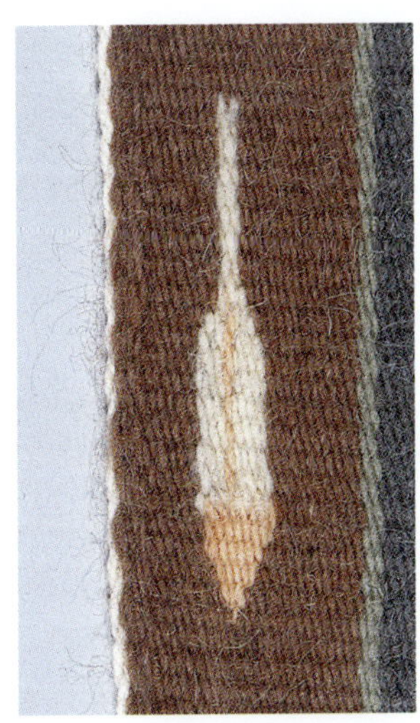

Figure 63. Close-up of a feather as a symbol signature in a Burnwater weaving by LaRose Bia.

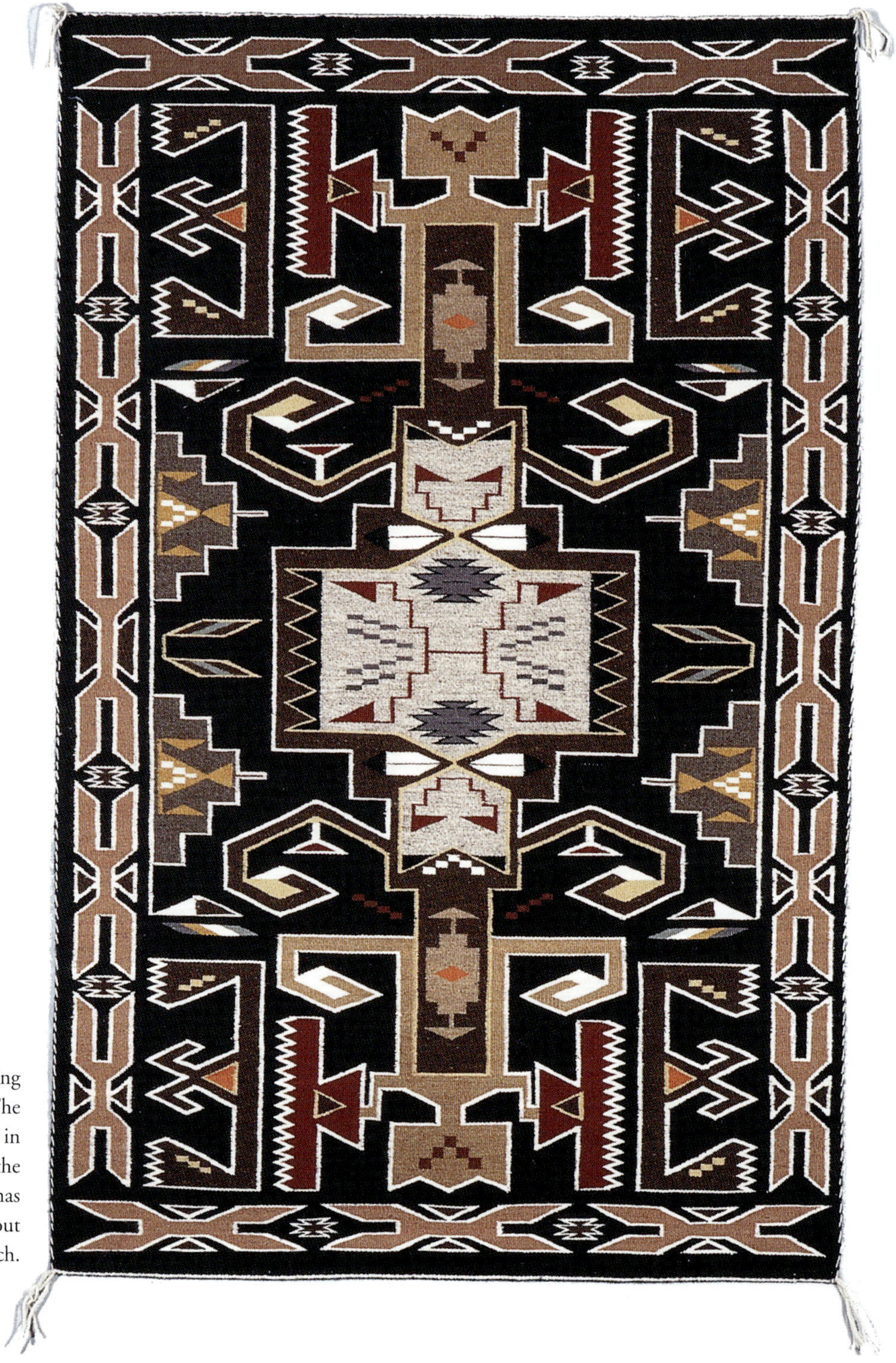

Figure 64. Teec Nos Pos weaving by Jason Harvey. 52 x 34 in. The black background is unusual in this region. In addition to the intricate pattern, Harvey has used a superfine weave of about 56 wefts per inch.

For centuries, women produced almost all Navajo weavings. At least one uniden-
tified male weaver worked in the nineteenth century. Hosteen Klah (mentioned earlier) wove in the early twentieth century. Until recently it was rare to find a Navajo
man at the loom. This was due in part to the fact that the Navajos considered weaving to be part of a woman's traditional knowledge and hence not a "manly" thing to
do. Many men who wove in the past sold their rugs under their wives' names to

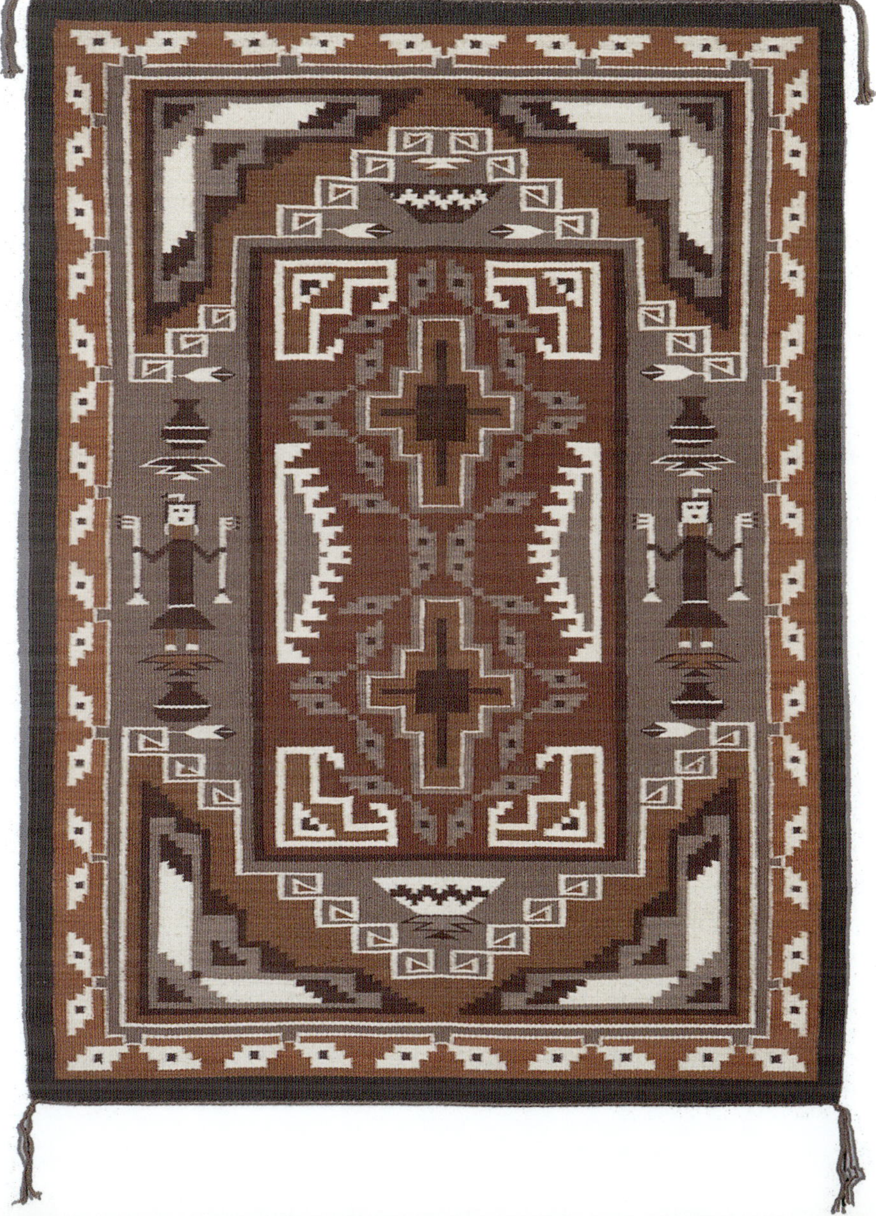

Figure 65. Burntwater weaving
with pictorial elements by Ruth
Nelwood. 46½ x 35½ in. Note the
Yé'ii basket, and pottery figures
along the sides, as well as the
rug-in-a-rug feeling of the piece.

avoid this stigma. Some still do so today, but more male artists are taking up weaving to bring in income for their families. In some cases, daughters have not carried on the tradition of their mothers, but sons have. Nowadays, most regions have several male weavers. One such weaver is Albert Jackson, now of Red Valley, Arizona. Being a male, he was not expected to weave but at about age six became interested in the process. He says, "One day while my family was away, I snuck some yarn to try to weave." When his grandmother and mother discovered his desire to learn, they agreed to teach him. He says that today female weavers respect his talents.

As with most Native American crafts, art has crossed gender lines. Katsina doll carving is no longer an all-male domain, and pottery is no longer an all-female one. More men are finding creative expression through weaving than ever before, and now most are willing to take credit for it. (FIG. 64)

Another important innovation in Navajo weaving at the end of the twentieth century was the movement away from strict regional stereotypes to a combination of elements from styles of many areas. Two-Grey-Hills–type textiles with Teec-Nos-Pos–type borders, storm-pattern weavings with sampler designs, and Burnt-water-style rugs with pictorial elements (FIG. 65)—all these are some of the many

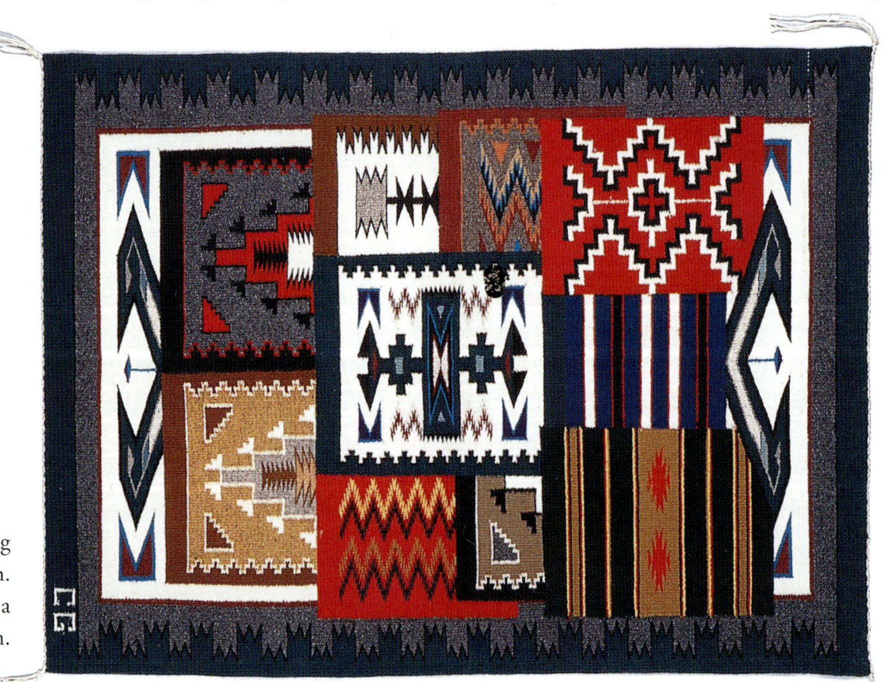

Figure 66. Sampler weaving by Cecilia George. 47 x 34 in. The background rug is a Teec Nos Pos pattern.

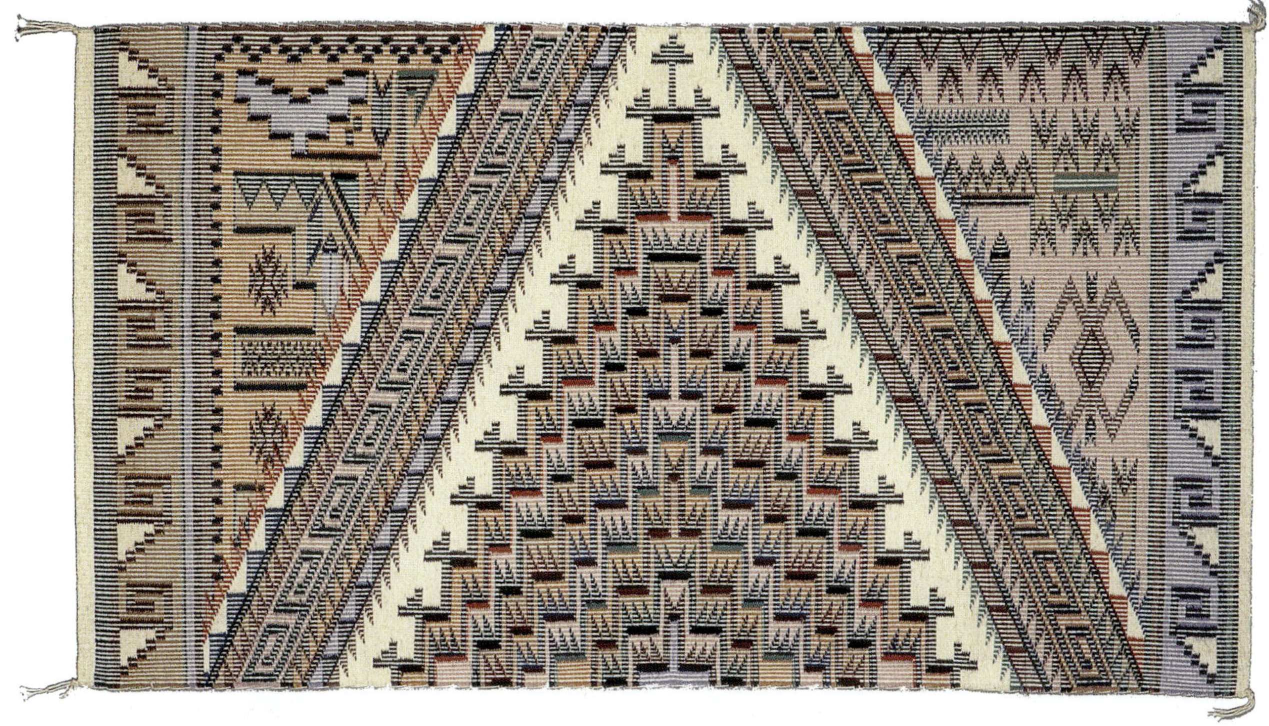

Figure 67. Raised outline "Blue Canyon" weaving by Lena Curtiss. 64 x 35 in. This textile includes the styles of at least three different areas.

varieties currently emerging. The advent of better highways and transportation has affected mobility and expanded the number of designs that weavers might see. For a prolonged time, weavers were exposed only to weavings of their own regional style. Now they can gather ideas from across the reservation. As with most artists, the desire to try something new is a strong one. Of course, today's innovations will become tomorrow's traditions.

Other stylistic changes are developing with some frequency and rapidity. In about 1990, Sarah Paul Begay (working from a concept of trader Bruce McGee's, then from Holbrook, Arizona) created a textile where the background rug had what appeared to be multiple small rugs laid randomly on top of it. The designs of the small rugs all overlapped one another so only portions of each were visible. Other weavers are now creating similar variations of this sampler rug. (FIG. 66)

In the "Navajo Weaving in the Twentieth Century and Beyond" section we mentioned the asymmetrical patterns in the Burnham area pictorial weavings. A different asymmetrical style was first woven by the late Larry Yazzie (YAH-zee), originally from the Blue Canyon area of the Western Reservation. Yazzie came

Figure 68. Mosaic weaving by Evelyn White. 48½ x 48½ in. White's outstanding piece won a blue ribbon at the 1996 Gallup Inter-Tribal Indian Ceremonial.

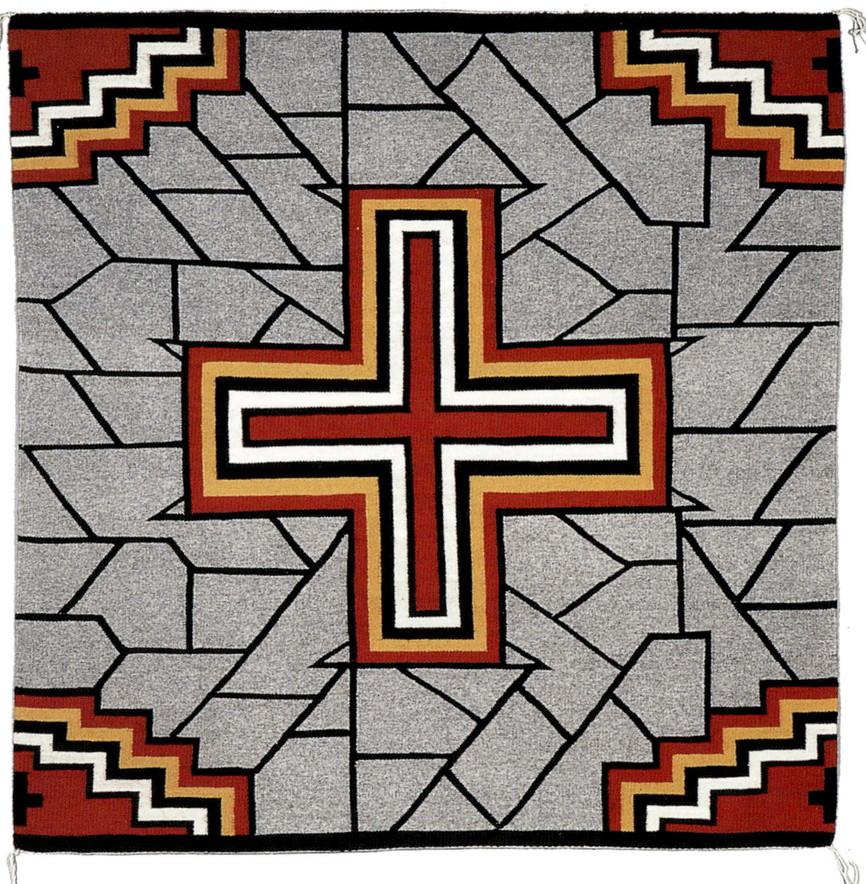

from a family with both male and female weavers. His style consisted of weaving different sections of the rug in different designs (storm patterns, Teec Nos Pos, Burntwater, etc.). He used the raised outline technique, but these variations have been called Blue Canyon rugs by their makers. Yazzie's sister, Lena Curtiss, continues this style of weaving today. Whether other weavers will break the strong Navajo tradition of symmetrical geometric rugs remains to be seen. (FIG. 67)

New styles of rugs are also emerging in southeastern Utah. One is the "mosaic" rug in which the central design element appears to lie on a fractured background. This idea was a collaboration between trader Steve Simpson, designer Susie Campbell Bell, and weaver Anita Hatathle in 1995. Other artists in the area are now making these as well. (FIG. 68) The other new creation from this area is the "mythology" rug, which shows scenes from Navajo myths and legends. The original concept came from trader Barry Simpson of Blue Mountain Trading Post in Blanding. They are being interpreted from the myths by Navajo graphic artist Damian Jim on a computer, a novel use of today's technology. Several talented weavers are currently producing them. The taboos that apply to weavers of sandpainting rugs are not applicable to these rugs because the scenes do not come directly from sandpaintings. (FIG. 69)

From the Western Reservation, two new weaving types have appeared. Dinnebito (dih-NEH-bih-TOE) black rugs were first woven around 1990. They use either traditional central diamond designs as seen at Ganado and Two Grey Hills or storm patterns, but with a black background. Rose Dan Begay first created them from an idea of traders Elijah and Jim Blair, now of Page, Arizona. (FIG. 70)

The unusual Spider Woman rugs are being woven primarily near Cedar Ridge and Bitter Springs, Arizona. Rena Mountain is credited with creating them in the late 1980s. The weavings have a square or rectangular hole in the center to represent the place of emergence that Spider Woman passed through to this world.

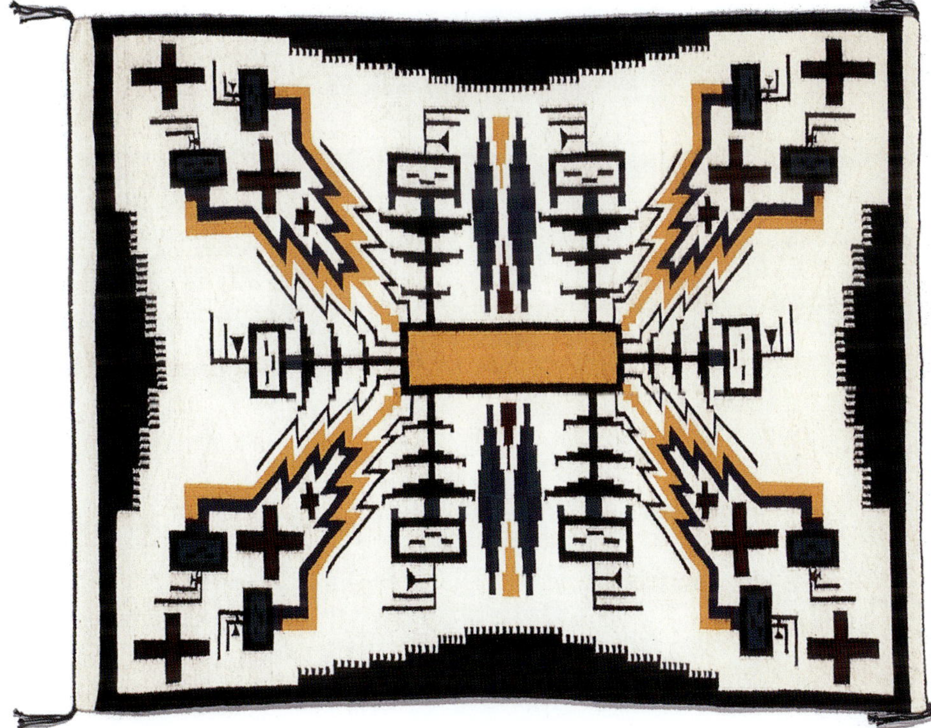

Figure 69. Mythology weaving by Christine Yazzie. 61 x 48 in. This example depicts the Corn Spirits.

Interestingly, some nineteenth-century rugs had small central openings called Spider Woman holes. (FIG. 71)

Another "new" technique is actually a return to an earlier style. Variegated colors running throughout a weaving hearken back to the variable colors and streaking seen in older weavings. At that time the color differences were caused by the use of multiple sources of wool and different dying practices. Today's variegation is very intentional as weavers float yarn in the dye bath so the part above the liquid absorbs less of the dye. A normal dyeing process would necessitate frequently rotating the yarn to achieve even dye application. (FIG. 72) Sometimes the yarn is tie-dyed with portions tightly wrapped in string to prevent the dye bath from penetrating and coloring that area. (FIG. 73)

With these many innovations, a greater appreciation and awareness of the artists as well as of the art have developed. Before the 1960s, most rugs were not even tagged with the weaver's name. Rugs were considered more of an anonymous piece of Native American decoration than a work of art by a specific Navajo individual. As better artists gained recognition for their workmanship and style, collectors began asking for their weavings by name. For example, many people now do not just ask for a tapestry weaving. They ask for a Barbara Ornelas or a Julia Jumbo

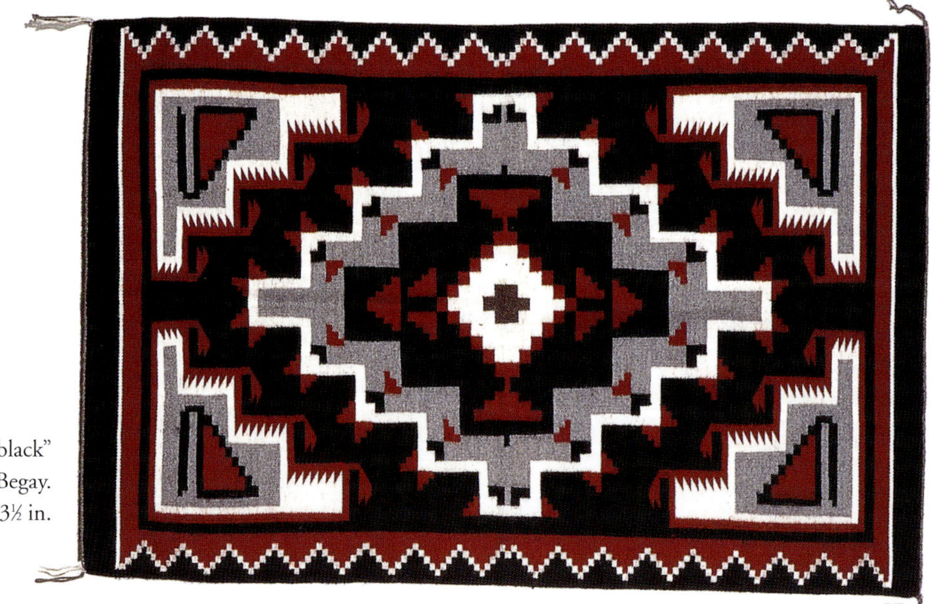

Figure 70. "Dinnebito black" weaving by Rose Dan Begay. 51 x 33½ in.

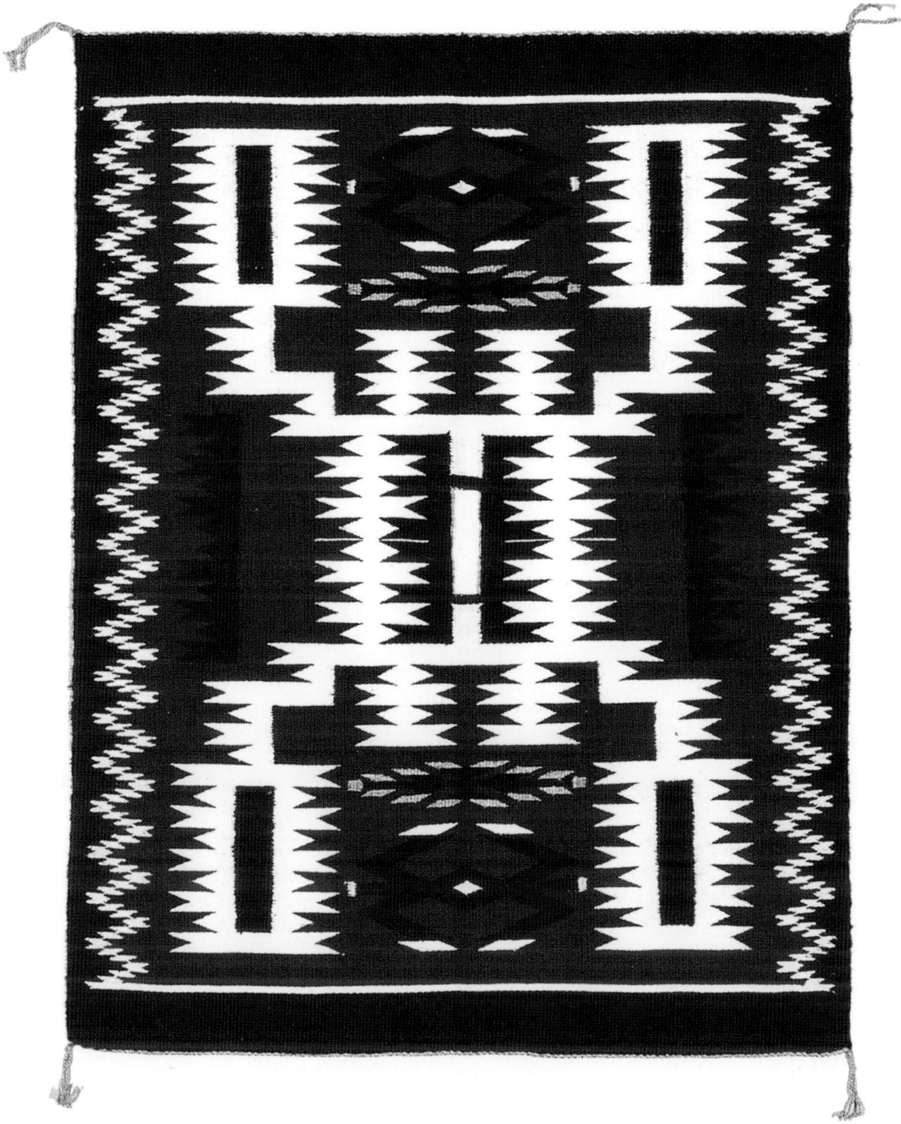

Figure 71. Spider Woman rug by Tomacita Sloan. 36 x 28 in. Note the rectangular opening (the emergence hole) in the center of the storm pattern.

tapestry weaving. Of course, any collector should remember the most important thing to look for is a quality piece, no matter who the weaver is.

So what is the future of Navajo weaving? Certainly we can expect to see more variety and inventiveness, even finer workmanship and more detailed combinations of patterns. Stephen Pickle states that now "a weaver might take design elements from several styles of weaving." With this increase in difficulty, higher prices for superior quality will be the inevitable result.

The biggest problem may be the decline in the number of weavers and weavings. Almost all traders note that fewer rugs are being made by fewer weavers every year. Trader Kent Morrow observes many weavers are getting squeezed out between entry-level weavers and major artists. Thus inexpensive pieces and extremely fine, collector-quality artwork sometimes dominate the market. When this happens, the majority of Navajo weaving artists are driven to get regular jobs,

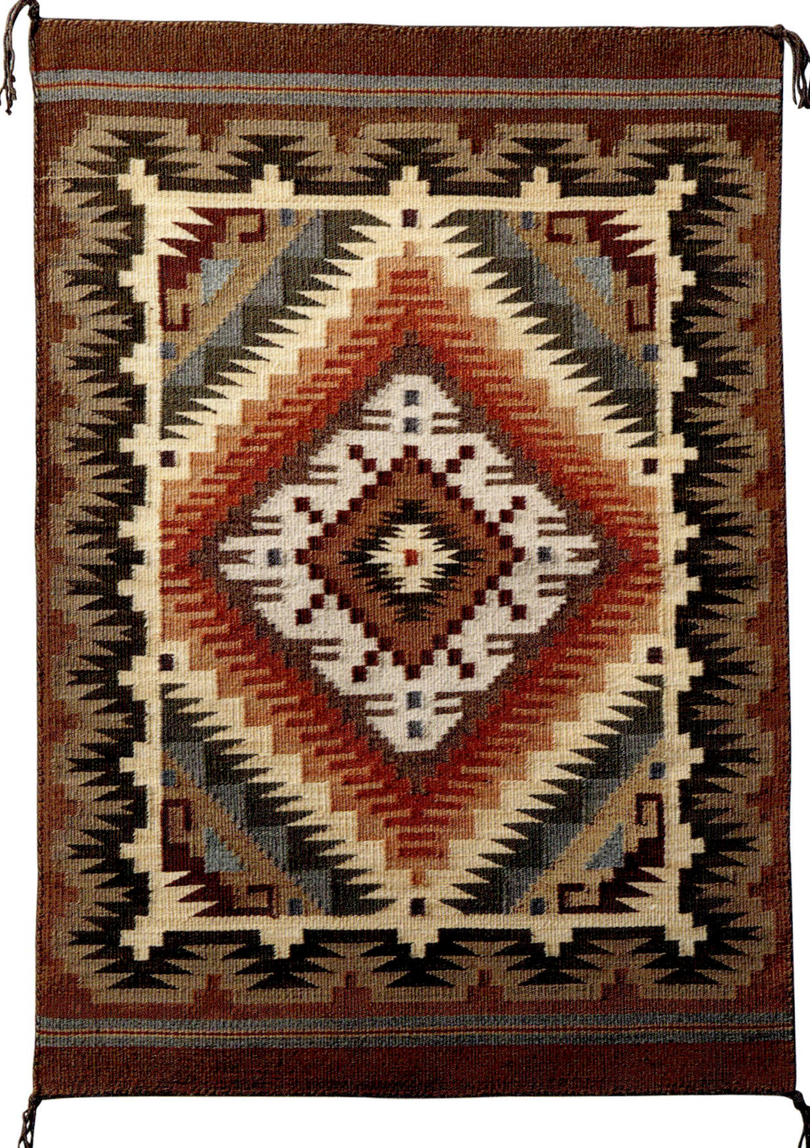

Figure 72. Burntwater weaving by Wanda Tracy. 32½ x 23½ in. This weaving is a good example of variegated yarns in home-dyed colors, which are quite subtle in the pastels of the Burntwater style.

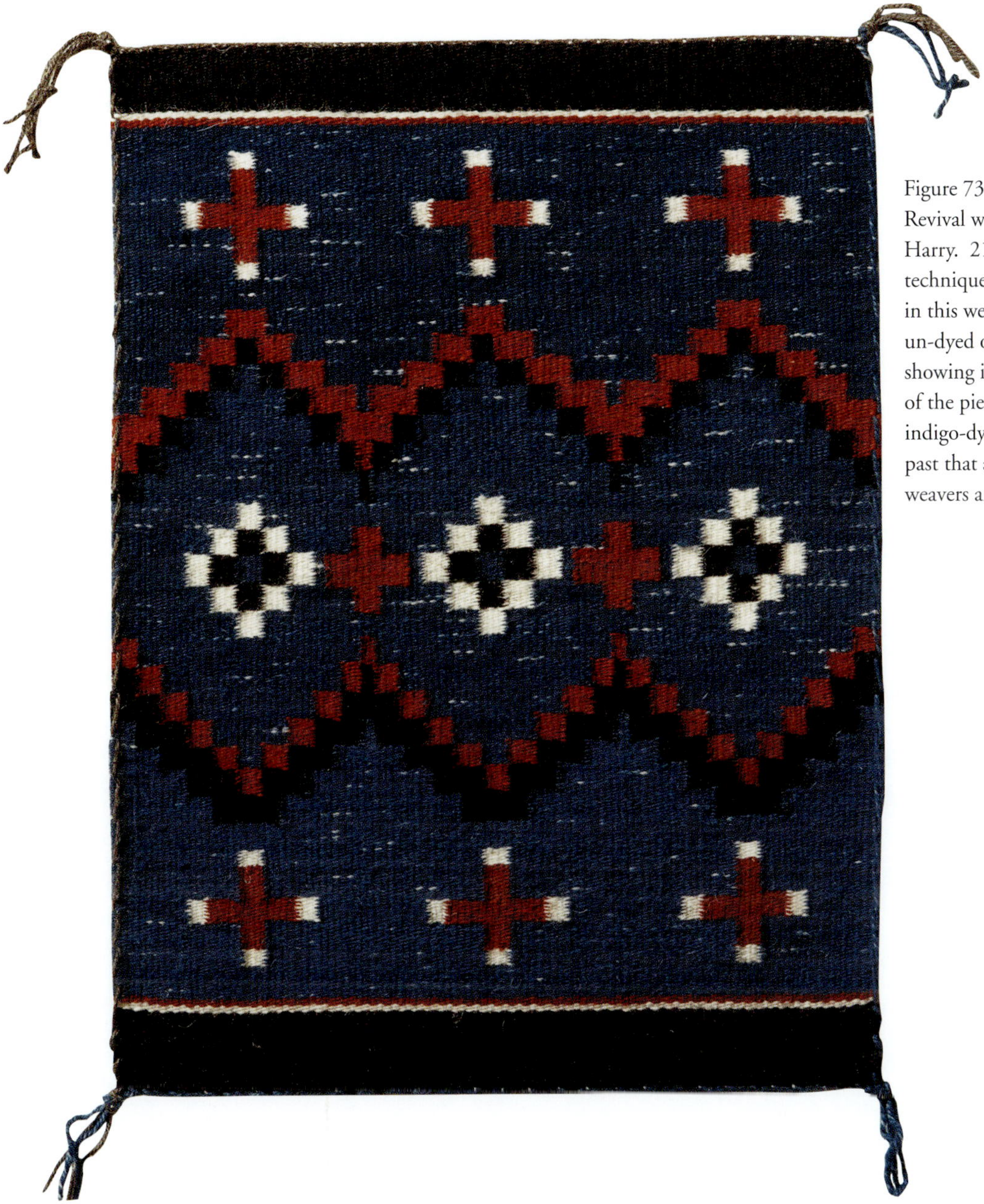

Figure 73. *Wearing Blanket Revival weaving by Nathan Harry.* 21 by 15½ in. The technique of tie-dying is shown in this weaving with areas of un-dyed or partially-dyed white showing in the blue background of the piece. The blue is indigo-dyed, an artifact of the past that a few contemporary weavers are reviving.

says Morrow, with weaving becoming a limited second income. As we have said, rug production is heavily market-driven. Even with rug prices as seemingly high as they are today, the vast majority of weavers still have difficulty making a living if weaving is their only reliable source of income. Unfortunately, most can even make more working at a fast-food restaurant than weaving.

One discouraging factor is that many shops choose to sell so-called Indian-design rugs from Mexico, the Orient, and other parts of the world rather than Navajo weavings. Other weaving cultures have their own unique patterns—reproducing Navajo ones strictly to make cheaper copies is ethically questionable. Potential buyers may not understand the difficulty and slowness of Navajo weaving compared to the ease and speed of techniques employed by other weavers. The qualitative differences between these weavings may also not be obvious to the uninitiated. Thus, inexpensive imitations compete directly with superior and more costly Navajo textiles. An unfortunate aspect of these knockoffs is that the seller may either intentionally misrepresent them or may encourage the customer to believe they are authentically Navajo by the use of terms like "Navajo design" or "Navajo style." The buyer should remember that the Navajos must live in our economy just as the rest of us do and cannot survive on the meager wages that workers in other countries do. It is also true that quality workmanship is available in virtually every price range of Navajo rugs, including even the least expensive pieces. However, a low price never excuses a poor-quality weaving.

Another issue is the perception that Navajo textiles are a craft rather than an art form. As Jed Foutz of Shiprock Santa Fe so convincingly puts it, "How can people spend so much on Anglo paintings and then complain about the prices of Navajo weavings, which take so much longer to produce?" Because of this, Foutz is concerned that younger weavers may not continue, and that the art could lose much of its current innovation.

Trader Bruce McGee of the Heard Museum Shop in Phoenix notes that for a few of the best weavers, the issue of money is less critical. For the weavers whose work is in greatest demand, traders may vie for these top-quality pieces in bidding wars. McGee recognizes that this is not true, of course, for the vast majority. Joe Tanner, a trader from Gallup, New Mexico, feels it is the trader's role to help the Navajo "come to the rug market with the best work they can do, so they will be able to meet their families' needs."

Bill Malone of Shush Yaz Trading Co. in Gallup, New Mexico, believes that inexpensive rugs may virtually disappear as younger weavers will not make "cheap rugs." He says weaving is headed more towards the upper end of the price spectrum, with only the best of the best getting top dollar for their work. Robert Inge-

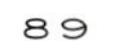

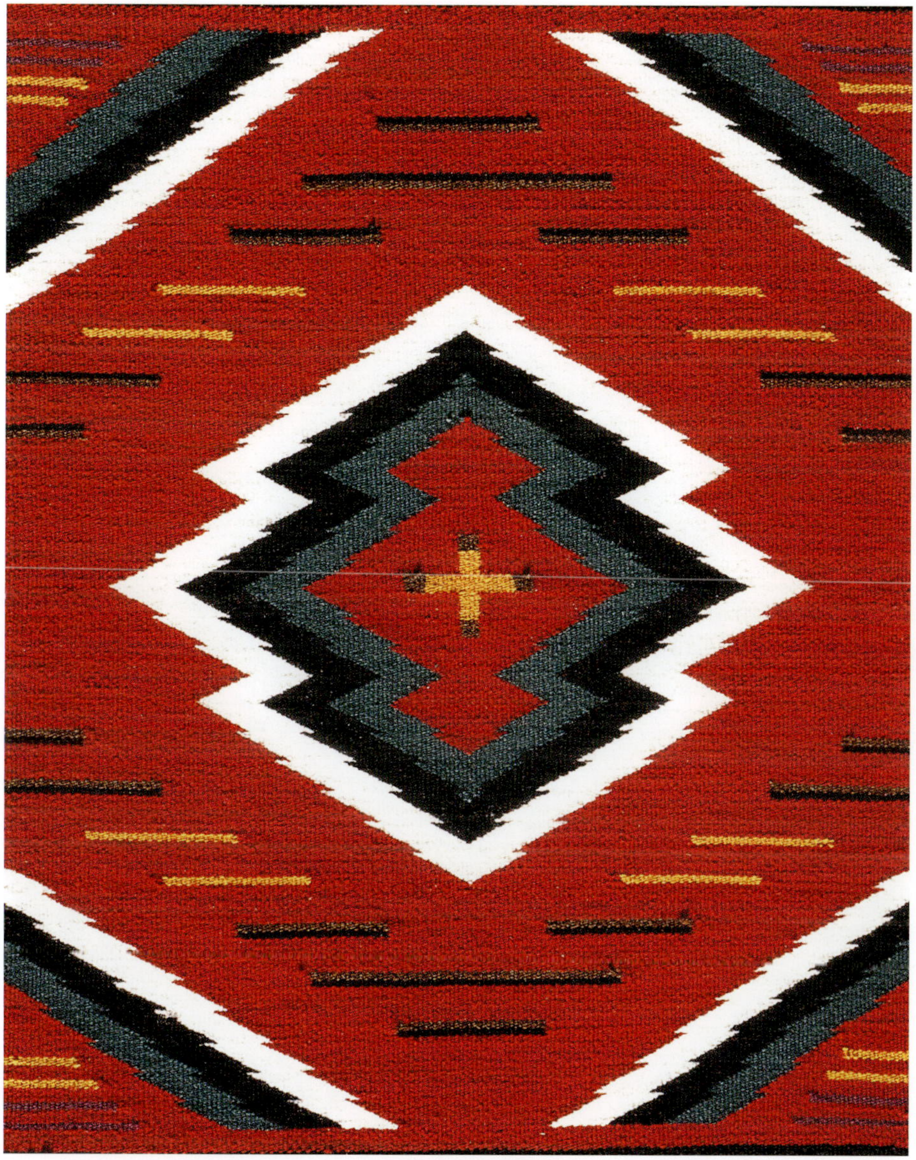

Germantown revival weaving by Priscilla Warren. 31 x 22½ in.

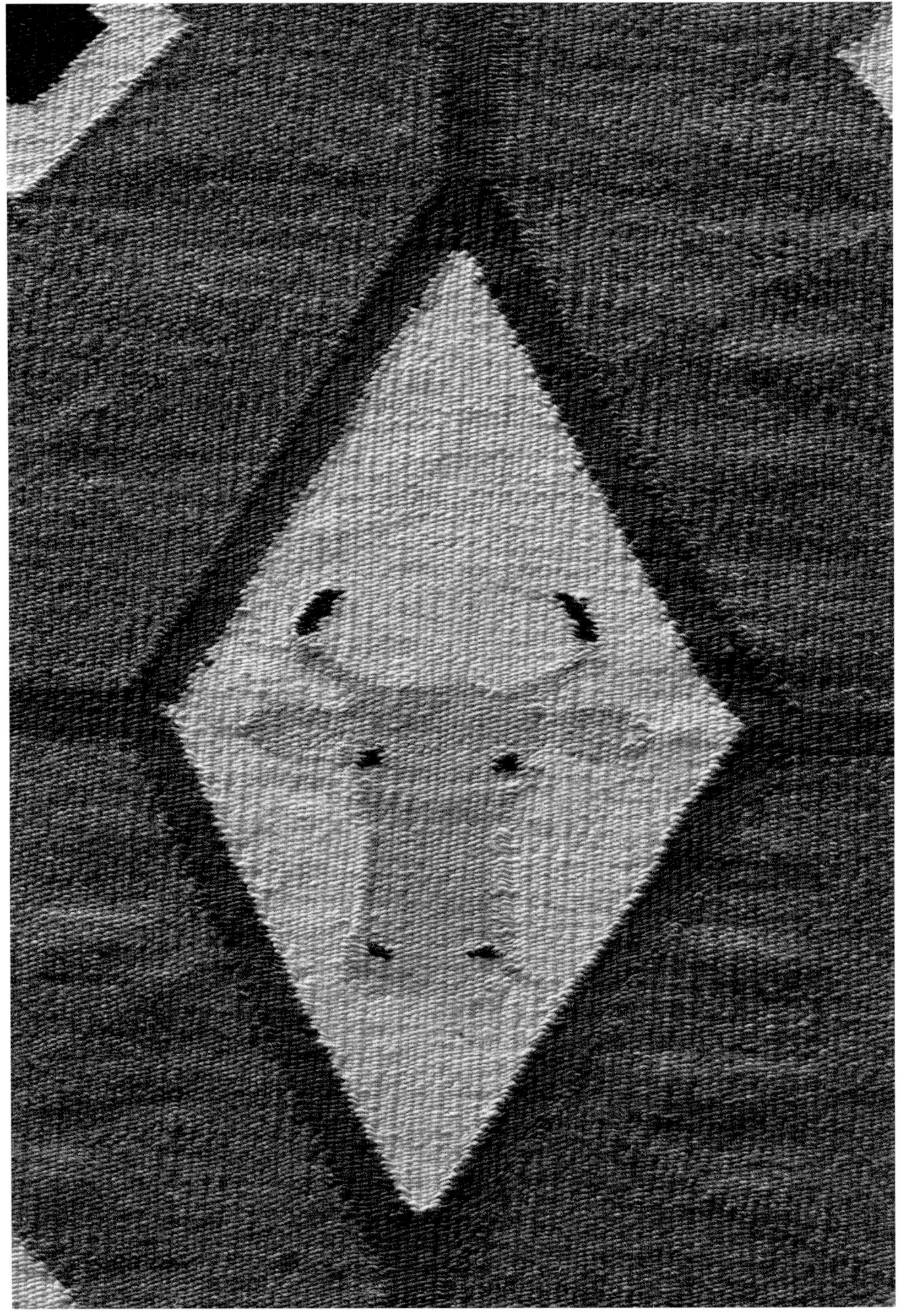

holm of Blair's Dinnebito Trading Post in Page, Arizona, agrees that the prices for better weavings will go up, while average-quality rugs will stay about the same. He expects to see rug production falling off more than 25 percent in years to come, especially among younger weavers.

Weavers, too, express concerns about where weaving is headed. Most of those we know are over forty years of age. Many seem to know a number of capable weavers, especially younger ones, who are not making or will not make rugs. Some young Navajos feel that weaving is old people's work.

In spite of the challenges, weaver Pearl Ben believes that the art of weaving will not die among the Navajos. She knows several Navajo in their twenties taking up weaving today. Albert Jackson points out that, like himself, more men are weaving than ever. Most weavers express hope that the art will be passed on to future generations, but there seems to be a sense of trepidation as well. As current weavers continue to age and younger ones do not replace them, the future of Navajo weaving may appear somewhat precarious. Fortunately, weaving classes in such places as Diné College in Ganado, Arizona, among others, are training new artists to continue the tradition.

We too feel that weaving will most likely continue. The look will change, perhaps dramatically, as it has many times in the past. The number of pieces produced may decline, but the quality may be even better. We believe this tradition of beauty and harmony will endure. An expression of this faith may best be voiced by Barbara Teller Ornelas. "I hope older weavers will be strong enough to teach younger weavers, since weaving is such an important part of being Navajo."

BIBLIOGRAPHY

Belikove, Ruth K. *The Rugs of Teec Nos Pos: Jewels of the Navajo Loom.* Albuquerque, NM: Adobe Gallery, 1994.

Brugge, David M. "Navajo Prehistory and History to 1850" in *Handbook of the North American Indians,* Vol. 10 (Alfonso Ortiz, ed.). Washington, DC: Smithsonian Institution, 1983.

Hedlund, Anne Lane. *Contemporary Navajo Weaving: Thoughts That Count (Plateau,* Vol. 65, No. 1). Flagstaff, AZ: Museum of Northern Arizona, 1994.

———. *Reflections of the Weaver's World: The Gloria F. Ross Collection of Contemporary Navajo Weaving.* Denver, CO: Denver Art Museum, 1992.

James, H. L. *Rugs and Posts: The Story of Navajo Weaving and Indian Trading.* Westchester, PA: Schiffer Publishing, Ltd., 1988.

Kaufman, Alice, and Christopher Selser. *The Navajo Weaving Tradition, 1650 to the Present.* New York: E. P. Dutton, Inc., 1985.

Kent, Kate Peck. "From Blanket to Rug: The Evolution of Navajo Weaving after 1880" in *Tension and Harmony: The Navajo Rug (Plateau,* Vol. 52, No. 4). Flagstaff, AZ: Museum of Northern Arizona, 1981.

———. *Navajo Weaving: Three Centuries of Change.* Santa Fe, NM: School of American Research Press, 1985.

Maxwell, Gilbert S. *Navajo Rugs: Past, Present, and Future.* (Revision by Bill and Sande Bobb.) Santa Fe, NM: Heritage Art, 1984.

McGreevy, Susan Brown. *The Image Weavers: Contemporary Navajo Pictorial Textiles.* Santa Fe, NM: Wheelwright Museum of the American Indian, 1994.

Mera, H. P., and Joe Ben Wheat. *The Alfred I. Barton Collection of Southwestern Textiles.* Coral Gables, FL: Lowe Art Museum, University of Miami, 1978.

Moore, J. B. *The Navajo.* Albuquerque, NM: Avanyu Publishing, Inc., 1986.

Reichard, Gladys A. *Navajo Religion: A Study of Symbolism.* Tucson, AZ: The University of Arizona Press, 1983.

Roessel, Jr., Robert A. "Navajo History, 1850–1923" in *Handbook of the North American Indians,* Vol. 10 (Alfonso Ortiz, ed.). Washington, DC: Smithsonian Institution, 1983.

Wheat, Joe Ben. "Early Navajo Weaving" in *Tension and Harmony: The Navajo Rug (Plateau,* Vol 42, No. 4). Flagstaff, AZ: Museum of Northern Arizona, 1981.

———. *The Gift of Spiderwoman: Southwestern Textiles and the Navajo Tradition.* Philadelphia, PA: The University Museum, University of Pennsylvania, 1984.

Wyman, Leland C. *Southwest Indian Drypainting.* Santa Fe, NM: School of American Research; Albuquerque, NM: University of New Mexico Press, 1983.

Weavers of Rugs Illustrated